THINKING
ABOUT
DEVELOPMENT

ENVIRONMENT, DEVELOPMENT, AND PUBLIC POLICY

A series of volumes under the general editorship of
Lawrence Susskind, *Massachusetts Institute of Technology,
Cambridge, Massachusetts*

CITIES AND DEVELOPMENT

Series Editor: Lloyd Rodwin, *Massachusetts Institute of Technology,
Cambridge, Massachusetts*

CITIES AND CITY PLANNING
Lloyd Rodwin

THINKING ABOUT DEVELOPMENT
Lisa Peattie

Other subseries:

ENVIRONMENTAL POLICY AND PLANNING

Series Editor: Lawrence Susskind, *Massachusetts Institute of Technology,
Cambridge, Massachusetts*

PUBLIC POLICY AND SOCIAL SERVICES

Series Editor: Gary Marx, *Massachusetts Institute of Technology,
Cambridge, Massachusetts*

THINKING
ABOUT
DEVELOPMENT

LISA PEATTIE
Massachusetts Institute of Technology
Cambridge, Massachusetts

PLENUM PRESS • NEW YORK AND LONDON

Library of Congress Cataloging in Publication Data

Peattie, Lisa Redfield.
  Thinking about development.

  (Environment, development, and public policy. Cities and development)
  Bibliography: p.
  Includes index.
    1. Economic development—Planning. 2. Technical assistance—Anthropological
  aspects. I. Title. II. Series.
  HD87.5.P4   303.4'4   81-15858
  ISBN 0-306-40761-2   AACR2

© 1981 Plenum Press, New York
A Division of Plenum Publishing Corporation
233 Spring Street, New York, N. Y. 10013

Printed in the United States of America

To ROBERT REDFIELD, of course

PREFACE

This book intends to be helpful to people—students and others—who are beginning to think about how to change the world via that activity we call development planning.

The issues of What is Progress? and How do we get it? are world-wide, although they appear in different form in societies like our own from the way they do in the Third World countries with their explicit development planning. These are two very big questions and have no easy or final answers. However, we can think about them in more rather than less effective ways. Thinking about them can be both a way of beginning to take action on issues of growth and change, and a way of understanding our own situation.

This book argues that thinking about development planning has gotten into trouble by dividing economy from society, and misconstruing moral-social-political issues as technical ones. Development planning has centered on economic planning, treating social issues as obstacles to growth, or as problems arising out of economic change. The book takes up a number of specific topics which enter into development planning—topics such as the organization of work, educational planning, family policy—to show how in reality the social and the economic, the moral and the technical, are one, and how thinking about policy in each area should therefore take an integrated perspective.

The subject for this book was handed to me by Lloyd Rodwin, who asked me to teach a course on "Social Aspects of Development." When I said I was not at all sure of what that meant, he said he was sure I would work it out. I have been trying to do so ever since.

William Doebele gave many helpful suggestions on the rewriting of a first draft. When I wanted to give it up, Peter Marris, Donald Schon, and Martin Rein encouraged me to go on and finish.

Finally, Lloyd Rodwin came into it again by boxing me into a promise to finish by a certain date.

Penny Johnson was a most competent typist and tactful editor.

LISA PEATTIE

Cambridge, Massachusetts

CONTENTS

Chapter 1 / THE MORAL ORDER AND THE TECHNICAL ORDER

This book is an attempt to look at economic development and development planning from an anthropological perspective. Because I am an anthropologist who works with development planners, it is also a work of self-examination, and inevitably bears the scars of autobiography. Therefore, I shall try to lay my cards on the table by giving a brief account of how I came to this self-examination and to think about development planning from an anthropologically illuminated point of view. But first, let me say what this book is not.

It is not an attempt to introduce the anthropologist's knowledge of culture and society as a corrective or counterbalance to economic thinking. Anthropologists have been expert at criticizing development planning for its destruction of

1

native communities and traditional values and for ineptness at taking cultural and social factors into account. I do not think that I can add much to this kind of criticism. And what is more important, and more autobiographical, I joined the planners long ago. Development planners are more my reference group than are anthropologists. But in that world, I am still an anthropologist. I find the anthropological perspective useful in thinking about development. Furthermore, I believe, and will try to argue, that the logic of history, the logic of development process, is bringing the thought of development planners closer to the perspective of anthropology. Therefore, I wish to show how the two lines of thought—that of anthropology and that of development planning—may be coming together, and to identify what seem to be the critical problems in their integration at the point of meeting.

My first encounter with development planning was in 1962. In that year, I went to Venezuela to join an interdisciplinary team in which a group of Americans—assembled by the MIT–Harvard Joint Center for Urban Studies—was working with Venezuelan professionals to plan for an industrial city on the Orinoco river and to develop the surrounding Guayana Region. I stayed for nearly three years as the project anthropologist. The project office was in the capital, but I lived on the site—a disorderly frontier city of some 50,000 people at the time—in a working-class, shantytown settlement. Every few weeks I went to Caracas to meet with the other project members, and, at irregular intervals, parties of planners came to the site.

When I went to Venezuela, I was almost completely lacking any experience or research on the issues of development, or, at least, the issues as framed by economists and planners. My father, Robert Redfield, was an anthropologist, and I had lived in small villages in Latin America as a child. I had studied social anthropology and engaged in research on American Indians and on American public schools. By my anthropologist father, and my training at the University of Chicago, I had been socialized into the traditions of community study and cross-cultural comparison; the only economics I ever had was an undergraduate introductory course in economic theory.

I found the planners of the new city on the Orinoco reading Walter Rostow and talking about how to create a city that would contribute to the national growth targets by having enough urbanity, and a sufficiently modern image, to attract American investment. I was to provide the developers with information on the customs and values of the people that would be relevant to their plans, and with some guidance on how to handle social problems connected with the urbanization process.

The way my colleagues defined my role as project anthropologist made me uncomfortable at the start, and, as time went on, more so. It appeared that anthropology had to do with "social problems" and with "customs and values"; it did not have anything to say about material interests. Here are three examples.

In the area of housing, the project architects wanted information about people's customs and lifeways in the domestic setting, and advice as to how such customs might affect appropriate housing design. I regarded the design issue as trivial compared with the issue of affordability, and both these issues as less consequential than who was to get access to the desirable locations and to profit from rising land values in the new city. The manipulated land and housing markets put the middle class into new subdivisions and relegated anyone who could not afford modern housing to that part of the city farthest from industry and without sewage and running water systems. On these matters, the anthropologist seemed to have no mandate to speak.

The social workers were deeply concerned about the prevailing "weakness of family structure" among lower-income people; marital unions, often consensual rather than legally established, broke up and reformed easily, so that at any given time many families were formally or, in effect, headed by women. The social workers, who regarded this as a cultural problem and thought that it lay in my domain, wanted to organize family-life courses. To me, the problem was more easily understood in the context of the instability of employment and the absence of any economic basis for marital collaboration. I thought the planners should reconsider an investment pattern that produced capital-intensive industry rather than jobs, and a productive mix that offered almost no jobs for women, other than domestic service and prostitution. However, once again, such comments seemed to be out of order.

Finally, we had a direct confrontation. At the request of some of the American planners, I inquired as to why, in a particular part of the city near the ferry dock, the shacks in which people were living seemed to be maintained in very provisional form, without being rebuilt or improved. Elsewhere in the city, people tended to upgrade their temporary shacks, over a period of time, into respectable, if modest, dwellings. The answer was that the Venezuelan planners had prohibited building in the city until planning was completed, and that in this particular area, because of its visibility, they were enforcing the ban with great stringency. (One father of three had several times been prevented by the police from digging a latrine.) I wrote a furious memo in which I proposed that the planners permit modest levels of self-improvement in areas not scheduled for immediate rebuilding by the public body. The head of the Venezuelan planning group told me to be an anthropologist and avoid issues that were none of my business.

In this growing frontier city, everyone wanted "development," everyone believed in progress, and no group more than those at the bottom of the system, who saw new opportunities opening up for themselves and their children. The planners spoke of "development." My neighbors in the shantytown spoke of "progress," of "the future of the worker," of "building the nation." The planners were reading Walter Rostow; my neighbors were reading the newspapers for reports of new firms coming to the city.

My own experience, in this environment made me feel that the anthropological role, at least as established around an intellectual focus on "culture" and "custom," was a prescription for irrelevance or worse. The attention to "culture" and "values" seemed a vain attempt to enforce a traditionalism that nobody wanted, to direct attention away from real issues of material interest, and to impede the critical attention that I wanted to direct on the role of the planners in reorganizing the world for the corporations.

During the years I spent on the project, I became progressively more and more dissatisfied. The planners, in their air-conditioned offices in Caracas, seemed to me further and further away from the social reality which I saw about me in the working-class neighborhood of the developing city, where my family and I were living, in a house with earth walls and a sheet metal roof, among steel workers and casual laborers. What I saw happening in the developing city fit less and less comfortably into the slots of "cultural barriers to" or "social problems connected with." On the basis of the social events around me, I gradually came to question the entire development strategy which the plans embodied.

It was a strategy that produced steel but few jobs; that organized the city for the advantage of foreign corporations, but made it difficult for local business people to get established; that concentrated power in the hands of a national elite and left local leaders and community members ignorant of what was being planned; that made some people rich, while appearing likely to leave many of my neighbors to pick up the "trickle down" of growth as an unskilled, intermittently employed subproletariat.

But I could not frame such issues in terms of "culture" or "customs and values." Progress, and development, was what everyone wanted, and none more than my hand-to-mouth neighbors whose perception of a world of opening possibilities was what gave life an intoxicating flavor.

Quite traditional anthropological research methods had led me to my criticisms of the planning. But my subject was clearly not culture, and if it was, as it appeared to be, development and development planning, then that seemed a topic for another group of specialists—the development economists and planners.

When I returned to the United States in 1964, the Joint Center for Urban Studies supported me for a year so that I could write something based on the Venezuelan experience. I set down my divergent reality in a small book, *The View from the Barrio*.[1] But at that time, I was painfully aware that I was basing my view on my own fieldwork. I had not really come to understand that other people had been thinking such

---

[1]Lisa Peattie, *The View from the Barrio* (Ann Arbor: University of Michigan Press, 1968).

thoughts, and my ideas seemed to me cranky and, more than likely, incorrect.

In the years since then, I have been exploring the body of theory and other research of colleagues and critics who could help me join my experience to other related experience. I have been reading and talking to professionals and academic people concerned with development issues, and treating these issues in my classes at MIT. I have looked at planning in Yugoslavia and Cuba; I have been back to Venezuela to see how that planned city has evolved; I have worked with planners in various developing countries. I have been trying to put that first experience in Venezuela into context.

This task, I see, is not complete; but this is a report on where I have gotten thus far.

Anthropology, in which I was trained, dealt with issues of development in two ways, neither of which would have seemed very relevant to development economists a few years ago, and neither of which, in fact, seemed very relevant to me when I first started working with development planners.

On the one hand, what the planners called "development" was for anthropology an aspect of the history of culture, of the story of the human species—the last few minutes of the long story that begins with paleontology and human evolution and goes on through prehistoric archaeology and the reconstruction of ancient civilizations. At this level, the findings of anthropology appear to be interesting only as historical background, holding nothing substantial of practical relevance for policymaking in the present.

On the other hand, anthropologists encountered development as they sought to record the cultures of primitive peoples—a myriad of designs for living, each with its own forms and patterns of meaning. Development was that process of technical change and colonial and commercial expan-

sion that was tending to destroy these various local cultures—
and sometimes the very tribal groups who were the bearers
of the cultures. In this context, the anthropologist experienced
development largely as destructive.

To national planners and most social reformers, this anthropological perspective came to seem excessively conservative and somewhat romantic. Change appeared to be inev-
itable. Often the people at the bottom, the peasants, the
tribals, seemed to want it, or at least much of what it could
provide. The issue seemed to be how to get *better* change:
more goods and services produced, and much more fairly
distributed. Useful anthropology seemed to be illuminating
issues of technical and economic change, not resisting change.

In rejecting the perspective of anthropology, I was specifically leaving behind the viewpoint of Robert Redfield, my
father. His thinking had centered around the values inherent
in the small societies that some called "backward" but that
he called "folk societies" characterized by "moral order"; this
he contrasted with the "technical order" of the market, the
business corporation, the managerial state in civilized societies. I wished to make the *technical* order work right; talking
about the moral order in backward societies seemed to me
inappropriate nostalgia. For, you will remember, I had
learned in Venezuela that the experience of development,
with all its pains and injustices, can be intoxicating: an open
future to be made, with hopeful possibilities.

It was, then, with something of a sense of shock, that,
in preparing a lecture on issues of development in the 1970s,
I found myself using my father's phraseology, "the relationship between the technical order and the moral order." The
subject was development planning—but I was thinking about
it like an anthropologist. It was the surprise of this experience
that made it seem appropriate to look at certain emerging

trends in thinking about development and to relate them back to stages of social and economic theory, which I had learned to think of as part of the history of ideas, and in the process, to find some new relevance in anthropology.

Now I prefer to move toward an integration of the anthropological perspective with the perspective provided within development planning. In considering the interaction between these two frameworks for thinking about development, I wish to adapt the terms from Robert Redfield's work: *the moral order* and the *technical order*.

The conceptualization comes out of Redfield's attempt to describe the essential ways in which the sort of small, isolated, homogeneous societies, which anthropologists traditionally studied, differed from the developed societies which he classed together as examples of "civilization."

> Technical order and moral order name two contrasting aspects of all human societies. The phrases stand for two distinguishable ways in which the activities of men are co-ordinated. [The phrase "moral order" is used to designate] all the binding together of men through implicit convictions as to what is right through explicit ideals, or through similarities of conscience. The moral order is therefore always based on what is peculiarly human—sentiments, morality, conscience—and in the first place arises in the groups where people are intimately associated with one another. . . . By a corresponding extension of another and more familiar term, all the other forms of co-ordination of activity which appear in human societies may be brought together and contrasted with the moral order under the phrase "the technical order." The bonds that co-ordinate the activities of men in the technical order do not rest on convictions as to the good life; they are not characterized by a foundation in human sentiments; they can exist even without the knowledge of those bound together that they are bound together. The technical order is that order

which results from mutual usefulness, from deliberate coercion, or from the mere utilization of the same means. In the technical order men are bound by things, or are themselves things. They are organized by necessity or expediency.[2]

In folk societies the moral order predominates over the technical order. It is not possible, however, simply to reverse this statement and declare that in civilizations the technical order predominates over the moral. In civilization the technical order certainly becomes great. But we cannot truthfully say that in civilization the moral order becomes small. There are ways in civilization in which the moral order takes on new greatness. In civilization the relations between the two orders are varying and complex.[3]

As to the trend of this relationship throughout history, I have one general impression. It is that the moral order begins as something pre-eminent but incapable of changing itself, and becomes perhaps less eminent but more independent. In folk society the moral rules bend, but men cannot make them afresh. In civilization the old moral orders suffer, but new states of mind are developed by which the moral order is, to some significant degree, taken in charge. The story of the moral order is attainment of some autonomy through much adversity.[4]

This is the view that I now see as central to the planning of development. In what we call "civilization," the moral order does not disappear; it becomes different; it is taken in charge. And one area in which it becomes different and is taken in charge is the area we call "development planning."

Here I should make something of a modification of Red-

[2]Robert Redfield, *The Primitive World and Its Transformations* (Ithaca: Cornell University Press, 1953), pp. 20—21.
[3]*Ibid.*, p. 24.
[4]*Ibid.*, p. 25.

field's dichotomy. The technical or practical and the moral or expressive or consensual appear as two aspects of the organization of human activities. However, we being the kind of creatures we are, a kind that symbolizes and interacts symbolically, the two aspects of order can never be actually separate. The technical order rests on a set of common understandings as to the right, the relevant, and as to the boundaries and structure of our practical concerns. The moral order of consensus and concern rests on ideas of practical interest.

Development planning, as an idea about taking society in charge, and as an activity with a number of subfields, is a part of the technical order of modern societies. But it is an aspect of the moral order as well.

Development planning deals with activities based in mutual usefulness: steel mills, roads, sewer systems, technical schools; in this aspect, it is part of the technical order. But planning is a social activity, vested in institutions that are held together and related to others through ties that rest on "implicit convictions as to what is right." The steel mill, the roads, the housing developments in the Venezuelan city, where I first encountered planning, were implicated with, the symbols of, and made possible by that very ideology of progress and nation building—"the future of the worker"—which constituted the ideological air we breathed.

The subject of economic development is inherently complicated and difficult to treat from a single perspective. Surely, it might be said, this is not such an intractable topic; there is, indeed, a substantial number of tightly organized books and articles on the theme. However, as circumstances and issues change, subjects have a way of changing their form as disconcertingly as the Duchess's baby in Alice's arms. The transformation of political and social institutions, the confrontations both within and between nations of the haves and the have-nots, and the struggle over scarce resources have made it more and more difficult to deal with the subject in any tidy framework, like that provided by economics. Once a subject is seen to involve worldwide and interrelated processes of economic and social transformation, and to be a way of designating the interaction of the human species with the natural environment, it becomes a topic so broad and complex that it is difficult to generalize. When one is confronted with such a subject, various strategies are possible. One is to divide the subject into subtopics. Another is to find a single theme or formula or "theory" that seems to express the central or basic character of the subject. Still another is to try to explore the subject first from one point, then from another, like a blind man who moves around the elephant feeling first the hindquarters, then the side, then the ears, and then the trunk.

It is this last strategy that I have adopted. The strategy of dividing the subject into subtopics like economic growth, social change, political development, I reject, in principle, as a way of effecting, for motives of convenience in intellectual administration, an arbitrary and confusing separation among processes inextricably interconnected. The second, or grandtheory, strategy I have rejected out of the necessities of my own nature; some people seem to be able to generate and to resonate to these general summaries, and to feel their understanding of the complex reality illuminated by them; but I am not one of them. So I have proceeded in the inelegant manner of starting first at one place and then at another, and of trying to develop each of these as a way into a complex whole.

Chapters 2 and 3 that follow this introduction each look at the general framework for thinking about development. First, I try to present what perspective anthropology can bring to the problem. Next, I look at the way economic development has been conceptualized in other social theory and try to show that the once-established division between "social aspects" and "technical issues" is no longer functional for the way the problem presents itself in planning and policy.

Chapters 4 to 7 treat some substantive areas of development planning.

In Chapter 4, I deal with the idea of "social planning" as one way of trying to get a more rounded and humane conception of and command over the development process, and show how this attempt produces its own ambiguities.

Chapter 5 explores the management of work by the Cuban Revolution to show how "societal planning" can rework a central economic institution to make it also central to political and social processes, and to suggest some of the issues that thus arise.

Chapter 6 deals with the family, an institution usually thought of as outside the realm of development planning, and attempts to trace the implications of economic transformation for family structure and to suggest some considerations that might be brought to bear on policy toward the family as an institution in a development context.

The final chapter of this group discusses a field—educational planning—which as "manpower planning" and "human capital development" may be thought to lie in economic planning, and in other aspects raises central issues in social planning.

Chapter 8 looks at the two ways of thinking about the "quality of life" which come, respectively, from the traditions of anthropology and those of economic planning. It tries to show that our current predicament demands that we draw from both traditions, even though they are, in their nature, extremely difficult to join.

This interpretation, however, presents a problem, to which I do not have a solution, that can be presented in two ways. As an intellectual problem, it implies: How do we develop a frame of reference and system of evaluation that encompasses both ways of looking at human experience? As an institutional problem, it means: What institutions might we develop that would make it possible for us to shape development to serve both kinds of needs? Neither way of asking the question seems to suggest a ready solution. Furthermore, the two are so related that we must answer both together; a "frame of reference" must serve an organization of interests.

But perhaps as we struggle with these intractable questions our way will become clearer.

Chapter 2 / ANTHROPOLOGICAL PERSPECTIVES

*The Human Species and
the Production of Culture*

To think about development as an anthropologist is first to place current developmental change as a set of recent events in the human career, as part of the history of our species on Earth. To have some visual imagery of what our human career has meant, it would be helpful to begin with the opening scenes of a stunning film entitled *The Hunters*, about the life of the Bushmen of the Kalahari. The film deals mainly with a giraffe hunt. When the film opens, we do not see man at all. We see the Kalahari, the dry grass, the little thorny trees, a small bird. When men appear, they move quietly, nearly naked, through the land. They are few, they are weak, and they make almost no mark on the natural environment. When these men find and spear a giraffe, they are unable to kill it at first. The animal escapes, wounded, and they track it for days. At the end, they at last surround the weakened animal, which yet looms unsteadily over them and their spears; they bring the giraffe down; they carry the meat home to camp; they divide it up. And, we are to understand, soon the hunters will have to begin again to hunt down another animal.

Once all men lived as these hunters of the Kalahari live. Indeed, for the better part of our history as a species, we lived like these hunters, puny animals compared with the game we hunted, moving through an environment in which we made minimal alteration. The grass bent under our feet and sprang back; we were one among the many species of hunting animals; we were few in numbers.

The difference between those men and ourselves is not of a biological nature, for those naked Bushmen of the Kalahari are of the same species as ourselves, that species *Homo sapiens*, of which all the presently existing races of man are members. The difference is not in intelligence, for, in so far as we know or can prove, all the branches of that single species are equally provided with the ability to learn and to invent. It is not even in a difference in the capacity to handle ideas through language, for of all the languages of man there is none that can be said to be truly "primitive," less fully human, than any other. The difference between those Bushmen and ourselves has to do with processes of social and cultural change, then, of which all human beings have the biological potential, although in not all cases has the potential run its course.

There is a biological basis for the distinctive human cultural potential. But for more than 99 percent of the duration of the genus *Homo*, our ancestors were gatherers and hunters; the entire species probably numbered no more than five to ten million people. The recent success of our species depends on technical discoveries, not on biological evolution.

So the answer to the question of how did we get to where we are now would seem to have two parts: first, how we came to be the kind of bipedal, tool-using, symbolizing primate we are biologically, and second, how that set of biological capabilities made possible the accelerating evolution of cultural change.

Man's tendency to invent may be the outgrowth of a manipulative, tool-using kind of primate nature, but the sequence of technological innovations characterizing our species and its history is unthinkable without language and linguistic conceptualization. Chimpanzees make and use simple tools. Man's ancestors probably made a variety of tools—of which the stone ones are all we now find—before human language was fully developed. But the technologies of even the most primitive of our own species are the outcome of communication and tradition, and technological research and development in the industrialized societies depends on intricately coordinated social organization and specialized expertise unthinkable without language. Human culture is cumulative, one idea building on another, one generation learning from its predecessors. Human culture is communicative and interactive, contacts between diverse groups stimulating new solutions and innovations. Human culture is inventive, characterized by breakthroughs, threshold crossings, accelerating rates of transformation. None of this would be possible without language and the symbolic abstraction that language makes possible.

One reason why man has been able to transform the earth is that the human capacity for symbolizing and for conceptualizing has made possible for the human species kinds of social organization impossible for any other animal. We are able, through specifically human kinds of symbolic processes, to organize social units which cover a very wide span. The flag, the national anthem, the ritualized processes of government, make possible larger, more enduring, and more complex forms of social organization, for which the structure of a troop of baboons, dependent as that is on continual visual and auditory contact, gives almost no analogue. The "moral orders" in which human beings live, from the scale of the primitive band of hunters to the modern nation-state, are expressions of the distinctive human capacity to think symbolically.

A related point—of no small importance when we come to the problem of sharing a limited planet—is that there seems to be very little use in discussing human problems of power and aggression in terms of the phenomena of dominance and territoriality in other animal species. It is not that we do not share many of the tendencies of these other species; we do. But we have, in addition, certain capacities that make our situation quite different. Because we have both the capacity for complex energy transformations and the capacity for complex social organization over distance, we human beings are able to aggregate resources over very wide territories. The capacity to use a large amount of resources (high technology) has as one of its aspects an institutional capacity to channel resources unequally through social organization. Power and inequality, applied to human affairs, refer to specifically human phenomena.

The processes through which the human species has come to dominate the earth are, therefore, both technical and social. It is not simply that man is an animal capable of complex tool invention; it is also that man is an animal capable of complex forms of organization with intricately coordinated division of labor serving to aggregate and channel the resources being exploited by the technical system.

The symbolizing capacity of the human species has made possible an extraordinarily rapid rate of change. Other animals become transformed through the slow operation of the processes of natural selection against natural mutations. We transform ourselves through culture so rapidly that it turns out that cultural change, now felt as outside our control, is transforming us.

> Scientific production has out-run our imagination, and the change in our civilization—in the practical means and techniques of life—has advanced with a gathered momentum of its own and outstripped the advance of our thinking. Our technological civilization, consequently seems to overtake and overwhelm us as though it were something foreign coming in on us.[1]

Indeed, our economic and social institutions seem to us almost as external and much more dangerous than the natural weather; nature may soak us to the skin or even produce an earthquake, but nature is unlikely in the long run to blow us up.

We live, therefore, in a world of human institutions. These institutions constitute our way of dealing with nature technically; they also shape the perceptual screen through which we understand both ourselves and the rest of nature. They are technique, but they are not merely technical; the technical is, for us, never the purely technical. Our ways of doing the business of life are styled, ornamented, attached to symbols, given meaning, and our arrangements for collab-

[1] Susanne K. Langer, "Scientific Civilization and Cultural Crisis" in *Philosophical Sketches* (Baltimore: Johns Hopkins University Press, 1967) p. 103.

orating in social groups are always dependent on, interpreted by, our symbol systems.

When we talk about development planning, then, we are talking about a kind of activity that is at the center of the human condition. Such planning is a specifically human capacity, which deals with specifically human difficulties in a specifically human way. This human activity of planning has to deal with an environment that we know to be largely of our own making, but that we know our institutions to be unable to control.

To think about development as an anthropologist is also to evaluate social and economic institutions not only as systems of meaning and value. Culture and society are not simply means: they are also ends. The society that a development planner would call "underdeveloped" may appear in the anthropologist's frame of reference in a very different light.

When Robert Redfield, drawing on earlier conceptualizations of Maine,[2] Tönnies,[3] and Durkheim,[4] tried to illuminate the differences between the societies of the developed and the underdeveloped world and the broad trend of human history, he did so by contrasting modern urbanized societies with that type of society that he called "folk."

> The folk society is small, isolated, nonliterate and homogeneous with a strong sense of group solidarity. . . .
> Behavior is traditional, spontaneous, uncritical and personal; there is no legislation or habit of experiment and

[2]Henry Sumner Maine (1861), *Ancient Law: Its Connection with the Early History of Society and Its Relation to Modern Ideas* (New York: E.P. Dutton, 1960).

[3]Ferdinand Tönnies (1887), *Gemeinschaft und Gesellschaft* [*Community and Society*], trans. Charles P. Loomis (East Lansing: Michigan State University Press, 1960).

[4]Emile Durkheim (1893), *De la division du travail social* [*The Division of Labor in Society*] (Glencoe, Ill.: Free Press, 1960).

reflection for intellectual ends. Kinship, its relationships and institutions, are the type categories of experience and the familiar group is the unit of action. The sacred prevails over the secular; the economy is one of status rather than of the market.[5] [In such a society] the ways in which the members of the society meet the recurrent problems of life are conventionalized ways . . . and these conventionalized ways have become interrelated with one another so that they constitute a coherent and self-consistent system. . . . The folk society exhibits culture to the greatest conceivable degree.[6]

The difference between this perspective and that of the development planner may be illuminated by quoting at some length an account of life in a "folk society" by a member of that society who remembered it, many years later, as it was in her youth, with overwhelming nostalgia. Here is the voice of an old Papago Indian woman, telling the anthropologist Ruth Underhill about her childhood:

> We lived at Mesquite Root and my father was chief there. That was a good place, high up among the hills, but flat, with a little wash where you could plant corn. Prickly pear grew there so thick that in summer, when you picked the fruit, it was only four steps from one bush to the next. And cholla cactus grew and there were ironwood trees. Good nuts they have! There were birds flying around, doves and woodpeckers, and a big rabbit sometimes in the early morning, and quails running across the flat land. Right above us was Quijota Mountain, the one where the cloud stands up high and white when we sing for rain.
>
> We lived in a grass house and our relatives, all around us on the smooth flat land, had houses that were

---

[5]Robert Redfield, "The Folk Society," *American Journal of Sociology* 52, no. 4 (January 1947) p. 293.
[6]*Ibid.*, p. 298.

the same. Round our houses were, with no smoke hole and just a little door where you crawled in on hands and knees. That was good. The smoke could go out anywhere through the thatch and the air could come in. All our family slept on cactus fibre mats against the wall, pushed tight against it so centipedes and scorpions could not crawl in. There was a mat for each two children, but no, nothing over us. When we were cold, we put wood on the fire.

Early in the morning, in the month of Pleasant Cold, when we had all slept in the houses to keep warm, we would wake in the dark to hear my father speaking.

"Open your ears, for I am telling you a good thing. Wake up and listen. Open your ears. Let my words enter them." He spoke in a low voice, so quiet in the dark. Always our fathers spoke to us like that, so low that you thought you were dreaming.

"Wake up and listen. You boys, you should go out and run. So you will be swift in time of war. You girls, you should grind the corn. So you will feed the men and they will fight the enemy. You should practice running. So, in time of war, you may save your lives."

For a long time my father talked to us like that, for he began when it was black dark. I went to sleep, and then he pinched my ear. "Wake up! Do not be idle!"

Then we got up. It was the time we call morning-stands-up, when it is dark but there are white lines in the east. Those are the white hairs of Elder Brother who made us. He put them there so we can know when day is coming and we can go out to look for food.

We crawled out the little door. I remember that door so well. I always crawled out of doors till long after I was a married woman and we stopped being afraid of enemies. Then we made houses with white men's doors. But this one was little and when we came out we could see the houses of my relatives nearby among the cactus, and the girls coming out of them, too, to get water.

Those girls had nothing on above the waist. We did not wear clothes then. They had strips of hand woven cloth in front and behind, tied around their waists with a string, for we did not know how to sew them together. Only deerskins the men know how to sew, but our people had traded this cloth from Mexico and we thought we were very fine. And with good red paint above the waist, it was fine. And warm too, but the girls did not put on their paint in the early cold morning. Then they had to work.

There was no water at Mesquite Root; no water at all except what fell from the clouds, and I am telling about the month of Pleasant Cold when the rains were long over. Then our pond had dried up. If we wanted to stay in our houses, the girls had to run for water far, far up the hills and across the flat land to a place, a good place for corn, and the water ran down to it from all the hills. A big water hole was there full of red mud. Oh yes our water was always red. It made the corn gruel red. I liked that earth taste in my food. Yes, I liked it.

The girls used to crawl laughing out of the houses, with their long black hair hanging to their waist, and they would pick up their carrying nets. Fine nets we used to have in those days, all dyed with red and blue. Shaped like a cone they were, with tall red sticks to keep them in shape. When the net was on a girl's back those red sticks would stand up on either side of her face. We used to think a pretty young girl looked best that way. That was how the men liked to see her.

I was too little to have a net then, or even clothes. But I used to help my cousins put the jars in their nets and to put little sticks between them so they would not break. The boys would stand laughing around and if there was one who was not a relative the girls would joke with him. They would throw gravel at him and run away, and once a girl said to one of my cousins: "Give me that male thing you have and I will put it between my water jars instead of a stick." So we called that man Between-the-Jar. Yes, that is how we joked in the old days.

Then the girls put the nets on their backs and if one

was married and had a baby, she put that on top in its cradle board. Some men went with them with their war arrows because there were Apaches in the land then. They all went running, running. If they saw dust in the distance that they thought was Apaches, they went dodging behind the giant cactus. You see, women had to run in those days. That was what saved their lives. Many hours they had to run, and when they came back every family had two little jars of water to last for the day. But we did not mind. We know how to use water. We have a word that means thirst-enduring and that is what we were taught to be. Why, our men, when they went off hunting, never drank at all. They thought it was womanish to carry water then.

My brothers went running off, too. Ah, how we could run, we Desert People; all the morning until the sun was high, without once stopping! My brothers took their bows and arrows and went far off over the flat land.

"Run," my father said to them. "Run until you are exhausted. So you will be a strong man. If you fall down tired, far out in the waste land, perhaps a vision will come to you. Perhaps a hawk will visit you and teach you to be swift. Perhaps you will get a piece of the rainbow to carry on your shoulder so that no one can get near to you, anymore than to the rainbow itself. Or maybe Coyote himself will sing you a song that has magic in it."

So they went off in their breechclouts and bare feet, running in the dark when they could hardly see the cactus joints on the ground and the horned toads—rattlesnakes there were not in that cool weather. One of my brothers did really have visions. The others used to come back without him, bringing jackrabbits for our dinner. The little boy would come in much later and never tell where he had been. But we found out long, long after, when he became a medicine man, that he had been lying dead out on the desert all those hours and that Coyote had come and talked to him.

When they were gone my mother would come

crawling out. She went to the little enclosure behind our house, made of greasewood bushes piled up in a circle and she got the pot of gruel. We always kept gruel in our house. It was in a big clay pot that my mother had made. She ground up seeds into flour. Not wheat flour—we had no wheat. But all the wild seeds, the good pigweed and the wild grasses. And corn, too! Some summers we could grow corn. All those things my mother kept in beautiful jars in our storehouse. Every day she ground some more and added fresh flour to the gruel and some boiling water. That pot stood always ready so that whoever came in from running could have some. Oh, good that gruel was![7]

Even allowing for a perhaps romantic anthropologist doing the recording, and for the nostalgia of old age for youth—I once had a sixty-year-old Colombian former bootblack tell me with much the same detail-savoring nostalgia about a boyhood spent largely on the Bogota streets—what sharp beauty this way of life has in the account of it. Every detail is relished in retrospect: the little fragile hut, the early morning light on the mountain, the taste of red earth in the corn gruel, the capacity to endure, to run, to do without water. The getting of water is useful, indeed indispensable, work; it is also a personal test, and an aesthetic experience, and a way of getting in touch with the natural and the supernatural—"Perhaps you will get a piece of the rainbow to carry on your shoulder." Did not this life have high quality? This is surely the type of folk society that "exhibits culture to the highest conceivable degree."[8]

Yet no set of economic indicators would give the primitive

---

[7]Ruth Underhill, *The Autobiography of a Papago Woman* (Memoirs of the American Anthropological Association, no. 46, 1936) pp. 5—7.
[8]Redfield, "Folk Society," p. 298.

Papago high marks. Housing was rudimentary, food was scarce, life was insecure, and the expectation of life was short. In this account, the very theme that gives life its flavor and central meaning was that of learning to cope with scarcity and danger. "We knew how to use water," the Papago woman says proudly.

If, indeed, the Papago woman clearly remembered in old age how things were in her youth, a set of social indicators built around "satisfaction" with various areas of life would have given her people a high rating. But the satisfaction remembered by the Papago woman was not the satisfaction generated by having more of some stock of generally recognized good things, relative to times past, or to other peoples in the present. It was the satisfaction of living a life of style and dignity within very tight constraints. There is the sense of completion in pursuing ends closely calibrated to the means available for attaining them; the pleasure of competence in coping; the comfort of bonding to others in the same collective endeavor; and the delight of experiencing the elements of daily life as linked together in a regular social rhythm, and as tied to the surrounding world of nature and the supernatural. This is the sort of thing that anthropologists have meant by "cultural integration"—and it is the lack of *this* sort of quality of life that the anthropologist Edward Sapir described when he saw the relatively affluent culture around him as "spurious" and judged that

> The American Indian who solves the economic problem with salmon spear and rabbit-snare operates on a relatively low level of civilization, but he represents an incomparably higher solution than our telephone girl of the questions that culture has to ask of economics.[9]

[9]Edward Sapir, "Culture, Genuine and Spurious," in *Selected Writings of Edward Sapir* in *Language, Culture and Personality*, ed. David G. Mandelbaum (Berkeley: University of California Press, 1949) p. 316.

The genuine culture is not of necessity either high or low, it is merely inherently harmonious, balanced, self-satisfactory. It is the expression of a richly varied and yet somehow unified and consistent attitude towards life, an attitude which sees the significance of any one element of civilization in its relation to all others. It is, ideally speaking, a culture in which nothing is spiritually meaningless. . . . A society may be admirably efficient in the sense that all its activities are carefully planned with reference to ends of maximum utility to the society as a whole, it may tolerate no lost motion, yet it may well be an inferior organism as a culture-bearer.[10]

The reader should not take away from all this the impression that anthropologists, in general, would now, or when these works were published, follow these examples in stressing cultural integration as against an interest in material well-being. A major review of Redfield's major work characterized the author—correctly—as "the defender of an approach which his colleagues have discarded,"[11] for lumping together such a wide variety of societies and cultures into the "ideal types" of "folk society" and "civilization." Oscar Lewis, restudying twenty years later a Mexican village studied by Redfield in 1927, brought to it a very different set of concerns, and found Redfield's picture, if not false, at least grossly deficient.

The impression given by Redfield's study of Tepoztlan is that of a relatively homogeneous, isolated, smoothly functioning and well-integrated society made up of contented and well-adjusted people. His picture of the village has a Rousseauean quality which glosses lightly over evidence of violence, disruption, cruelty, disease, suf-

[10]*Ibid.*, pp. 314—315.
[11]George Peter Murdock, review of *The Folk Culture of Yucatan*, by Robert Redfield, in *American Anthropologist*, 45 (1943), 133—135.

fering and maladjustment. We are told little of poverty,
economic problems, or political schisms.[12]

The nostalgia which in Redfield's writing had been apparent, for those simpler societies which, in his words, "exhibit culture to the greatest conceivable degree," seemed to
Lewis a romantic evasion of economic and political problems.

When Indonesia became independent, one of the first
acts of the new government was to expel the anthropologists,
not only for their association with Dutch colonial rule, but on
the basis of their association with a positive evaluation of
cultural tradition. Many anthropologists would see the Papago woman's story as romanticizing, and urge their fellow
professionals to focus on issues of poverty and economic
inequality.

From this perspective, discussions of the "quality of life"
and of the loss of culture constitute a luxury to be indulged
in by materially satiated elites in developed—perhaps over-
developed—countries. Nor does it go down well, to someone
who is struggling to modernize the economy of some poor
underdeveloped country, to be told by well-fed intellectuals
that in the process of bringing about economic growth, his
people are likely to lose a certain traditional beauty of cultural
style and a certain inner serenity that have characterized the
preindustrial way of life in their country. He might even argue
that the underfed peasants were not so much serene as tired
out. He might go further; he might say something like, "Yes,
now that you people have everything you want—and some
of what you have we should like, too—you tell us not to

---

[12]Oscar Lewis, "Tepoztlan Restudied: A Critique of the Folk-Urban Conceptualization of Social Change," in *American Essays* (New York: Random
House, 1946), p. 38.

bother with it at all, just so we shall leave you in peace with your accumulation. We can see through that easily enough."

Nevertheless, it turns out that there are a number of reasons why issues of the quality of life cannot expediently be left for later in thinking about economic development.

It has become clear that not only the fact of economic growth but the way in which that growth takes place or is deliberately brought about is bound to affect almost every aspect of life, from the meaning of work to the structure of the family. The development process, therefore, is one that, in each instance where it takes place, shapes the quality of life. Decisions about development policy are decisions about the quality of life, whether they are thought of in that way or not.

Furthermore, once distribution becomes a central issue of economic policy—and it certainly has become a central issue—other questions naturally follow. Questions of distribution naturally raise issues less conventionally treated as part of economic policy—issues of power and of social institutions, issues of political and social consensus, issues, generally, of the shape of society. Questions of distribution can never be treated easily, simply as practical ones, in the way the attempt has been made to treat issues of growth; distributional issues are clearly normative as well. Once we come to scrutinize the distribution problem, we are bound to find ourselves discussing the question: What sort of society is it that we want?

There is another factor, which we are just now beginning to become familiar with, that is bound to force forward issues of the quality of life: this is the growing concern with what goes, so far, under the heading of "ecology." We are coming to realize that resources are limited, and that man is still a part of nature who must live as a species within certain natural limits. We are beginning to press against some of those limits. We know now that the rest of the world cannot press forward into economic growth on the pattern of Europe and the United States; there simply are not enough resources to support the entire world's population in that style—even if, seeing our example, the rest of the world should wish to follow us. The developed world is not a model; it is a group of peoples that have taken more than their share and have used it carelessly. We could imagine the process taking place again in one or two countries—but after that? No, the earth cannot support the whole human race in the style to which Americans have become accustomed. This means that we must rethink the problem from the ground up.

In sum, the contribution of the anthropological perspective to thinking about development seems to involve three major themes.

One is the conception of development as a recent aspect of the career of the human species, and a focus on the place of the human species in nature.

Another is the understanding that man is both producer and consumer of culture. It follows that culture and its range of symbolization is both the means and the end of the development process. The institutions through which we carry out what we call "economic growth" are social institutions with a cultural aspect. The consequences of this economic growth also have to be evaluated as to the kind of culturally human world they imply.

Finally, there is the understanding that all human societies have an aspect of "moral order" and an aspect of "technical order," but that the two are interpenetrated.

Chapter 3 / DEVELOPMENT ECONOMICS AS A SOCIAL STUDY

In the way we look at the development process we have perhaps circled around to a position of vantage something like that from which we started. It has been a wide circle and, like any reasonably well-conducted journey through rough country, an educational one; we do not see the world in the same terms as we did when we began, and, as the world at which we look has become very different from that of a century ago, the vision we have is bound to be very different indeed from that of the theoreticians of that time. Yet there are similarities, and in some ways the themes that come into focus now are more like those of an earlier time than they are like the problems that preoccupied economic and social theorists of fifty or even twenty years ago.

In the process, it may be argued, thinking about development has come to bring forward a set of issues that make relevant the sort of ideas brought forward from anthropology in Chapter 2. The rather economistic way of thinking about development, characteristic of the 1950s, has given way to an understanding, still groping for a proper language, that "economic development" refers to complex processes of societal transformation. This, in turn, gives relevance to the anthropologist's view, which understands economic processes as embedded in social institutions, and social institutions as the vehicle for creating value and meaning. The "technical order," which was the topic of development economics, requires the support of the "moral order" and has goals that must be thought of in terms of quality of life, not simply as an aggregate of material production.

The second theme that seems to link current understanding of development with an anthropological perspective is what is usually referred to as "ecological issues." As development has involved a rapid increase in human population, combined with an accelerating use of resources, thinking about development has had to move beyond a concern with increasing the production of material goods to a concern, as yet not clearly reflected in practice, for maintaining a balance between human activities and the natural environment. The problem is also seen to be one that must be managed on a global scale. Thus, it appears not inappropriate to see "economic development" in the framing of the career of the human species. The "ecological crisis," in turn, raises new issues in the relationship between technical order and moral order and places new demands on the capacity of human beings to create new forms of moral order, integrating the members of a species scattered over the globe and separated both by conflicts of interest and by varying kinds of localized orders.

The way in which current thinking about development has come to resemble, in some ways, more the thought of the commentators on its earlier stages than the thought of intervening decades, may be illustrated first with respect to the thought of the late eighteenth- and early nineteenth-century economists—Adam Smith through John Stuart Mill.

Classical economics was, of course, an attempt to understand what was happening to Britain as it underwent, for the first time in human experience, that cataclysmic transformation that we call the Industrial Revolution, and also an attempt to predict, on at least a general level, the future that was in store.

On reading the classical economists now, one is struck first by the broad general questions being asked; the issue is the transformation of society, through the working out of economic processes which are thought of, for the most part, on the model of natural laws. Adam Smith's *The Theory of Moral Sentiments* (1759), in which he discussed the nature of the social sentiments that make a viable society possible, preceded in time, and was part of, the same set of interests that produced his now better-known inquiry into the source of economic progress, *The Wealth of Nations* (1776). Even in *The Wealth of Nations*, although treating such topics as the division of labor, taxation, land rent, the origin and use of money, and the relationship between urban and rural development, Smith saw nothing incongruous in a long disquisition on the history and the proper forms of education for youth. Malthus, Ricardo, and Marx all dealt with the process of development in terms of the distribution of shares between land, labor, and capital, and how these would interact in a system that must change its structure over time through the playing out of the interaction. Marx's version was, of these, the most frankly political, but the point of view was not unique. "Land," "labor," and "capital" were for all these men clearly *landlords, workers,* and *capitalists*—economic classes—and what they were modeling was, in fact, the changing structure of society, with the dynamic in economic forces.

The great classical economists of the late eighteenth and early nineteenth centuries also sounded a theme that fits better into current economic thinking than it would have into the intellectual climate of a decade or so ago in their attention to the issue of resources, and their concern with the potentially self-limiting character of economic growth.

Indeed, to a modern reader, classical economics is characterized by an extraordinary pessimism. Despite a faith in human rationality well entrenched since the Enlightenment, and despite the utopian imagery of the Owenite socialists, the major British economic thinkers saw the development process as one that would combine a growing national prosperity with a subsistence-level existence for the mass of the population, and which was, in time, bound to grind itself to a halt like a self-destroying machine.

Malthus's conception of a natural system of interaction between population and resources which would tend always to press toward subsistence, and which made attempts to relieve pauperism more than likely to aggravate the conditions such programs were trying to alleviate, was not subscribed to completely by other thinkers. But, as a general structure of thought, it colored thinking about economic policy for generations.

Indeed, of all the miseries experienced by the working classes of England during the Industrial Revolution, not the least must have been the absence of any ideology of national progress such as those now characteristic of the developing nations of the present.

> The process of industrialization is necessarily painful. . . . But it was carried through with exceptional violence in Britain. It was unrelieved by any sense of national participation in communal effort, such as is found in countries undergoing a national revolution. Its ideology was that of the masters alone.[1]

The economic thought of the period told workers that raising wages would simply cause population to expand, pushing wages down to subsistence levels again.

Further, even this painful process of growth was seen as inherently self-limiting, and as tending, in the most optimistic view, toward a stationary state, and in the more pessimistic view, to radical deterioration. The importance of "land" in the classical system brought the finiteness of resources into the center of their systems of analysis. Even the relatively optimistic John Stuart Mill saw emigration and free trade as providing a "temporary breathing time" in which the cultural conditions for population control might develop sufficiently to make possible a relatively tolerable stationary state freeing men from "crushing, elbowing and treading on each other's heels."[2]

The conceptualization of an inexorable process of technical progress—what we now call development—based on the unfolding of science and the spread of rational organization, was the work of a group of nineteenth-century social thinkers, the fathers not of modern economics but of modern sociology and anthropology. They saw humanity as the center

[1] E. P. Thompson, *The Making of the English Working Class* (New York: Penguin Books, 1968), p. 486.
[2] John Stuart Mill (1878), *Principles of Political Economy* (Toronto: University of Toronto Press, 1965) p. 754.

of a great historical drama: the transformation of the human condition from a kind of social life governed by interpersonal sentiment and collective symbolism to a life organized by market exchange, technical rationality, and mutual utility. Robert Redfield, with his contrast between folk society and civilization,[3] was the inheritor of this nineteenth-century tradition established by Henry Maine,[4] with the evolution from a society of status to one of contract; Tönnies, with the evolution from *gemeinschaft* to *gesellschaft*[5]; and Durkheim, with the contrast between societies characterized by organic and those characterized by mechanical solidarity.[6]

Thus there came to be established the intellectual framework for thinking of development as a species-wide or worldwide process of modernization, involving the spread of rationality and individualism, powered by transformation of the technical order, and bearing in its train the loss or submergence of that sphere of meanings that Redfield had identified as the moral order.

To complete our century's frame for thinking about development, it only remained to separate the realm of the economic from the other social sciences and to develop a way of thinking about economic process as part of the technical order. It required John Marshall's thought and the development of marginal analysis to shift the focus from the evolution

[3]Robert Redfield, "The Folk Society," *American Journal of Sociology* 52, no. 4 (January 1947).
[4]Henry Sumner Maine (1861) *Ancient Law: Its Connection with the Early History of Society and Its Relation to Modern Ideas* (New York: E. P. Dutton, 1960).
[5]Ferdinand Tönnies (1887), *Gemeinschaft und Gesellschaft* [*Community and Society*], trans. Charles P. Loomis (East Lansing: Michigan State University Press, 1960.)
[6]Emile Durkheim (1893), De la division du travail social [*The Division of Labor in Society*] (Glencoe, Ill.: Free Press, 1960.)

of the economy, as a whole, over time to individual decision making, and to market conditions and prices for particular commodities and sectors at a certain time.

The "stationary state" and society-as-a-whole receded from attention. The way was free for that open-ended, implicitly optimistic mode of thought that has so characterized the approach to development issues in the first half of the twentieth century. What could be further from the image of the "stationary state" than that of a "take-off into self-sustaining economic growth"?[7]

"Development economics" as it appeared in the fifties and sixties differed strikingly from the body of thought that had gone before not only in its methodology but in its whole way of framing the issues.

In the first place, development was thought of not as an aspect of the career of the human species as a whole but as a policy issue for individual national governments, mediated to a degree by a set of international institutions. The human race was seen as painfully divided between the haves and the have-nots, and as characterized by particular national development problems.

Furthermore, development was thought of as an economic process, not as societal transformation. Society and culture were relevant to the economic process, of course. "Social factors" entered as constituting obstacles to development, or as representing a sphere of social problems created by the strain of development on a traditional order.

Furthermore, the technical order and the moral order had, in effect, been divided into different spheres of competence; the economists were developing models of economic

[7]W. W. Rostow, *The Process of Economic Growth* (New York: W. W. Norton, 1962).

development firmly centered on the technical order, whereas anthropologists and sociologists were busy describing, analyzing, deploring, and, to some extent, suggesting ways of alleviating the stresses in specific moral orders brought about through the process of development. When culture and society came into the thinking of economists, they were as factors shaping the components of the technical order. The economists worried about how to develop entrepreneurship, a disciplined labor force, a pattern of economically productive investment, in nations whose existing cultural and social patterns seemed inappropriate to maximizing the pursuit of material prosperity.

The economic historian Walter Rostow, for example, whose book on "the take-off into self-sustaining economic growth" set the tone for a period of thinking in development economics a good deal more optimistic than the present, works with a set of cultural and social "propensities" that, given magnitudes, constitute the framework for a modeling of economic process. These are the propensities: (1) to develop fundamental science, (2) to apply science to economic ends, (3) to accept the possibilities of innovation, (4) to seek material advance, (5) to consume, and (6) to have children. For the take-off to occur,

> it appears necessary that the community's surplus above the mass-consumption level does not flow into the hands of those who will sterilize it by hoarding, luxury consumption or low-productivity investment outlays. Second, as a precondition, it appears necessary that institutions be developed which provide cheap and adequate working capital. Third, as a necessary condition, it appears that one or more sectors of the economy must grow rapidly, inducing a more general industrialization process; and that the entrepreneurs in such sectors plough

back a substantial proportion of their profits in further
productive investment, one possible and recurrent version of the plough-back process being the investment of
proceeds from a rapidly-growing export sector.[8]

Rostow's idea of the processes involved in the take-off
(and indeed, the very idea of a take-off) have been criticized
as excessively simplistic, and the whole discussion is very
much abstracted from the real political-economic-social process in any society. Yet there is a lot of sociology here, in the
form of those propensities or social-cultural factors. However,
they have been neatly bracketed into means and instruments,
named and designated, and not to be examined by the economist, for a process of economic progress taken as the overriding aim of social activity.

A frame of reference like this can easily be translated into
a large field of policy-focused research on social and cultural
obstacles to (or conditions for) economic growth, and social
scientists have responded to the challenge, producing a vast
output of books, articles, and whole journals in the area (see
especially *Economic Development and Cultural Change*). This literature deals both with social organization and with individual behavior and motives, often with the two together or with
one or the other being the focus of attention.

From this perspective, social and economic change may
be seen as a problem of behavior modification on the grand
scale.

David McClelland, stimulated by Max Weber's *The Protestant Ethic and the Spirit of Capitalism*, described the problem
as lying specifically in the existence or nonexistence of a particular kind of motivational structure, and "need for Achieve-

[8]W. W. Rostow, *The Stages of Economic Growth: a Non-Communist Manifesto*
(New York: Cambridge University Press, 1971), pp. 49—50.

ment." But then, since such basic aspects of character structure as a concern with "doing well" seem to be acquired,
generally early in life, within the family. . .⁹ a sphere rather
inaccessible to public intervention, the practical problem becomes that of developing programs of ideology, education,
and preferment, and organization which can maximize the
"need for Achievement."

On the other hand, Banfield's study of a South Italian
community identifies a cultural trait—the "ethic of amoral
familism"—as the basis of a kind of social organization re-
tarding development, and concludes, remarkably
pessimistically:

> There is some reason to doubt that the non-western
> cultures of the world will prove capable of creating and
> maintaining the high degree of organization without
> which a modern economy and a democratic political or-
> der are impossible. There seems to be only one important
> culture—the Japanese—which is both radically different
> from our own and capable of maintaining the necessary
> degree of organization.[10]

In a somewhat more positive vein, Everett Hagen has
seen as the basic requirements for the transition to economic
growth

> (a) fairly widespread creativity—problem-solving ability
> and a tendency to use it—and (b) attitudes towards man-
> ual technical labor and the physical world such that the
> creative energies are channeled into innovation in the

[9]David C. McClelland, *The Achieving Society* (Princeton: D. Van Nostrand Co., 1961).
[10]Edward C. Banfield, *The Moral Basis of a Backward Society* (New York: Free Press, 1958), p. 8.

technology of production rather than the technology of
art, war, philosophy, politics or other fields.[11]

From this he goes on to hypothesize the sorts of social
change that can tend to produce these sets of mind—in general, those in which an old elite loses its status respect, setting
in train certain processes within families of members of the
affected group.

The issue of economic entrepreneurship in itself has at-
tracted a substantial number of writers in a rather less psychological vein who have joined Schumpeter's theory of social
deviance with the sociological concept of the "marginal man"
to look at the social conditions for the emergence of this kind
of economic behavior.[12]

At a more general level, sociologists inspired by Talcott
Parsons have tried to delineate the conditions and processes
through which a society might change from one characterized
by social roles of a certain type (functionally diffuse, ascribed,
with particularistic criteria) to one in which roles tended to
become functionally specific, achieved, and subject to universalistic criteria. Here again, the theory of social deviance
came to the fore; the problem was seen essentially as that of
breaking through "the cake of custom," into modernity and
change. The moral order is seen simply as an obstacle to
development. Development is seen as a societal process, indeed, but as a societal process that obliterates the very ties
of community, consensus, tradition, and collective ritual,
which, to an earlier age, would have seemed the essence of

[11]Everett E. Hagen, "How Economic Growth Begins: A Theory of Social
Change,"*Journal of Social Issues* 19, no. 1, (January 1963): 20—34. See also
idem, On the Theory of Social Change (Homewood, Ill.: Dorsey Press, 1962).
[12]See A. Gerschenkron, *Economic Backwardness in Historic Perspective* (Cambridge: Harvard University Press, 1962).

society. Development is seen as the process by which the relations of "necessity and expediency" that we have identified as the technical order come to dominate thoroughly the relations binding persons "through implicit convictions as to what is right," identified as the moral order.

It is this way of looking at issues of development that I would argue no longer seems appropriate, even to economic planners. Certainly one of the factors that brought us to our current position in thinking about development is the role of government. Development in the countries of the Third World characteristically refers not to a process but to a project, a national project under the mandate and initiative of the state. One of the more interesting peculiarities of thinking about development must surely be the circumstance that economists, seeing the world in terms of supply and demand, utility curves, and "market forces," are the counselors to the new states in these nation-creating and economy-building projects.

Adam Smith thought of government as necessary to economic growth in certain basic but very minimal roles: for defense, for the legal protection of property without which contractual relations could hardly be enforced or investment take place, and for supplying certain public institutions and public works "of such a nature that the profit never repay the expense to any individual or small number of individuals."[13] Aside from this, its contribution was generally that of standing out of the way while private economic actors, pursuing each his self-interest, produced a greater stock of wealth for all. Government, in this view, seems to play no role in developing a new moral order on a wide scale: it simply has a

[13]Adam Smith, *The Wealth of Nations* (New York: The Modern Library, 1937), p. 681.

minimal technical role as a kind of peacekeeper and national housekeeper.

It became quite clear that this image of the process would never do in the nations that were trying to develop economically in the twentieth century. Gunnar Myrdal points out that the technical order is not self-managing.

> Economists now generally endorse the opinion that the underdeveloped countries need much more planning and state intervention if, under very much more difficult conditions than the now-developed countries ever faced, they are to have any chance of engendering economic development. Statesmen and officials from the rich and progressive Western countries have also been led to take the same stand on those other countries' behalf when the matter has been up for discussion and resolution-making in international organizations—although it is very apparent that they often had their fingers crossed when swearing on the strange bible.[14]
>
> As economic development cannot be expected to come by itself, planning becomes a precondition for development, not, as in the Western countries, a later consequence of development and all the other changes which accompanied it. The underdeveloped countries are thus compelled to undertake what in the light of the history of the Western world appears as a shortcut.
>
> All this follows as a consequence of the fact that planning is being applied at an earlier state of development, and of the further fact that their conditions for development are so much worse that this seems rationally motivated. It is also a part of the logic of the underdeveloped countries' situation that their programmatic planning should be comprehensive and complete, not pragmatic and piecemeal as in the Western countries. In

[14]Gunnar Myrdal, *Beyond the Welfare State* (New Haven: Yale University Press, 1960), p. 15.

principle and in theoretical approach, planning antici-
pates public policies. It does not grow out of the necessity
to coordinate such policies as have already been
initiated."[15]

In this connection, the kind of large-scale moral order that we
call nationalism may be seen as a precondition for planned
change in the technical order. "The development of nationalism in a nation can strongly support and reinforce pro-
grammes of economic and social change and thus the relationship between nationalism and economic development is
a causal one."[16]

Or Rostow:

As a matter of historical fact a reactive nationalism—
reacting against intrusion from more advanced nations—
has been a most important and powerful motive force
in the transition from traditional to modern societies, at
least as important as the profit motive. Men holding
effective authority or influence have been willing to up-
root traditional societies not, primarily, to make more
money but because traditional society failed—or threat-
ened to fail—to protect them from humiliation by
foreigners.[17]

So the moral order at the national level appears to be a
vehicle for development of the technical order. There have
been produced, with this perspective, a number of studies of
the political context of economic growth and of the role of

[15]*Ibid.*, pp. 122–123.

[16]James C. Abegglen, "The Relationship between Economic and Social Programming in Latin America," in *Social Aspects of Economic Development in
Latin America*, Egbert de Vries and José Medina Echeverría (eds.) (UNESCO,
1963), p. 264.

[17]W. W. Rostow, *The Stages of Economic Growth: A Non-Communist Manifesto*
(Cambridge: Cambridge University Press, 1960), p. 26.

government institutions, both at the national level[18] and with respect to particular sets of planning and development entities at more local levels.[19]

All these ways of thinking about "the problem of underdevelopment" locate the relevant conditions, and the obstacles to be overcome, within the backward society itself. But suppose that the social and cultural arrangements that eventuate in low material productivity are the consequence of overriding processes outside the particular society in question, or, if of independent origins, are of relatively minor importance, compared with more powerful forces at an international level? A societal transformation perspective may lead not to the nation and the national state but to the global political economy. Just as Marx saw the poverty of the English workers as an integral part of the system that produced riches for the rising capitalist class, so the underdevelopment of certain nations can be seen as the reverse side of the international system that produces wealthy nations.

> The rule of monopoly capitalism and imperialism in the advanced countries and economic and social backwardness in the underdeveloped countries are ultimately related, representing merely different aspects of what is in reality a global problem.[20]

[18]E.g., Gabriel A. Almond and James S. Coleman, *The Politics of the Developing Areas* (Princeton: Princeton University Press, 1960); J. B. Powelson, *Institutions of Economic Growth: A Theory of Conflict Management in Developing Countries* (Princeton: Princeton University Press, 1972).

[19]E.g., Richard P. Taub, *Bureaucrats Under Stress: Administrators and Administration in an Indian State* (Berkeley: University of California Press, 1969); Lloyd Rodwin (ed.), *Planning Urban Growth and Regional Development: The Experience of the Guayana Program of Venezuela* (Cambridge: M.I.T. Press, 1969).

[20]Paul A. Baran, *The Political Economy of Growth* (New York: Monthly Review Press, 1957), p. 250.

It becomes possible to speak of underdevelopment not as a failure to develop but as societal development of a certain kind: of "the development of underdevelopment"[21] through a variety of specific mechanisms, including political control over the colonized societies by the industrialized ones, the terms of trade as between nations exporting raw materials and those exporting primarily manufactured goods, the effects of technologies derived from and responsive to the already developed nations, and the capital-transfer role of the international corporations.

If we look at the problem as one of the structure of the global political economy, is the concept of a moral order still useful? I believe that it is, in several ways. In the first place, I think that, just as the problems of managing the complex technical order of an industrializing economy have made the kinds of moral order we call "ideology" and "nationalism" more, rather than less, salient, so our capacity to develop a workable way of managing the technical order at the global level will depend on our capacity to develop forms of moral order that support that integration. Second, the steadily increasing scale of technical organization in a more and more interdependent global system seems to create a kind of backwash demand for moral order on the level closer to people's lives—the ethnic group, the community, the neighborhood.

Yet there is still another way of looking at the relationship between technical order and moral order. In the foregoing discussion, as in the theories on which it is a commentary, the technical order dominates. All these varying perspectives on development and underdevelopment, whatever their anal-

[21]Andre Gunder Frank, "The Development of Underdevelopment," in *Latin America Underdevelopment or Revolution* (New York: Monthly Review Press, 1969), pp. 3–17.

ysis of causality, whether the problem is seen as lying within the underdeveloped society or in the relationships between societies, are alike in one way: all of them treat society as a means, adequate or inadequate, for the maximization of material well-being, taken as a fairly generalized or aggregated goal—in effect, the sort of goal that can reasonably be represented by the statistical exercises that go into computing a gross national product. In other words, the technical order dominates the definition of goals as well as of means.

In the last few years, there has been a growing disquiet with this way of looking at the problem, which comes, in part, from a growing concern with the way in which production is distributed. A programming advisor of the World Bank recently raised some uncomfortable questions and concluded that "a high growth rate has been, and is, no guarantee against worsening poverty and political explosions." Previously, the author of a respected book on development,[22] who had claimed that it was futile to argue about dividing the pie until development had produced more pie to divide, was now shocked by the break-up of the state of Pakistan over issues of unequal development into rethinking the problem.

> What has gone wrong? We were confidently told to take care of the GNP and poverty will take care of itself, that a high GNP growth target is the best guarantee for eliminating unemployment and redistributing incomes later through fiscal means. Where did the development process go astray? My feeling is that it went astray in at least two directions. First, we conceived our task not as the eradication of the worst forms of poverty but as the pursuit of certain high levels of average income. . . . We also went wrong in assuming that income distribution

[22]Mahbub ul Haq, *The Strategy of Economic Planning: A Case Study of Pakistan* (Karachi, Oxford: Oxford University Press, 1966).

policies could be divorced from growth policies and
could be added later to obtain whatever distribution we
desired. . . . Where does all this lead? It leads us to a
basic reexamination of the existing theories and practice
of development. . . . First, the basic problem of development should be redefined as a selective attack on the
worst forms of poverty. . . . Second, the developing
countries should define minimum or threshold consumption standards that they must reach in a manage-
able period of time, say a decade. . . . Third, the concerns for more production and better distribution should
be brought together in defining the pattern of development; both must be generated at the same time; the
present divorce between them must end. . . . Fourth,
and this is implicit in the third, employment should become a primary objective of planning and no longer be
treated as only a secondary objective.[23]

When an officer of the World Bank—which is, after all,
very much a bank, albeit a rather peculiar one—makes the
point strongly, it seems to mark some sort of turning point
in thought, underlined when the President of the World Bank
in a speech a few years later defined as "the central task of
development itself: the reduction—and ultimately the elimi-
nation of absolute poverty."[24] Indeed, the concern with employment and with distribution appears to be becoming a sort
of new orthodoxy, developed in economic models of earnings
and employment in various sectors during the development
process, in the employment-focused country studies of the
International Labour Office, and in a number of general
summaries.

[23]Mahbub ul Haq, "Employment and Income Distribution in the 1970s: A
New Perspective," *Development Digest*, ix: 4.
[24]Robert S. McNamara, "Address to the Board of Governors" (Washington,
D. C., September 1, 1975).

But the establishment of this line of thought suggests a further development. The concern with distribution may be thought of as a disaggregated version of the old production goals; instead of the gross national product, we have a set of measures showing the material gains for each segment of a given population. Or it can be thought of as a property of a whole social system: as equality. When one writer on Cuba says that "Egalitarianism may be considered a nonmaterial output of the Cuban productive system alongside more familiar material outputs such as butter and barbering,"[25] he opens up the possibility of evaluating that system, and others, in terms of other, analogously treated, "nonmaterial outputs." In this case, not only is the moral order a vehicle for development in the technical order, the technical order becomes a means to the moral order. Perhaps we have always known, at bottom, that the technical order was a means; but we may now find ourselves confronting it as such more directly than has been our custom for some years.

There is another force pushing our thought in this direction besides the political demands for greater equality in the sharing of production. This is the growing awareness that we are beginning to encounter certain physical limits in the development process. The development process, far from being that open-ended movement toward "progress" which it once appeared to some, proves to have a certain self-limiting character. It has made it possible for more people to survive on the earth; it has dealt to many of those people a much larger quantity of physical resources; and it has given those who have not yet been recipients of similar quantities of resources the aspiration, and, at times, the demand for their

[25]Robert M. Bernardo, *The Theory of Moral Incentives in Cuba* (University: University of Alabama Press, 1971), p. 152.

share. It has become clear that it is not possible for the people of the United States, for example, to go on indefinitely increasing their standard of living, at least as represented by material goods, at the rate they have done in the last fifty years; and much less is it possible to support the rest of the world in the same style. Kenneth Boulding claims that we are moving out of the epoch of "cowboy economics" in which consumption and production are both seen as good, and success is measured by throughput from the "factors of production," to a "spaceman economy" in which the basic concern is with stock maintenance and the allocation of resources within limits that are not continually being pushed back.

> The essential measure of the success of the economy is not production and consumption at all, but the nature, extent, quality and complexity of the total capital stock, including in this the state of human bodies and minds included in the system.[26]

In the United States, the stream of toasters, hi-fis, electric toothbrushes, cement mixers, skimobiles, haircurlers, ashtrays, and other material goods, vast as it is, now constitutes well under half the output of the economy. Will not the movement into spaceship economics make nonmaterial goods an even more important part of the output of economic systems? Thus it appears that though the concern with ecological issues and the concern with equalizing distribution may make conflicting demands on our system of management, both push us to question the management strategies that have left the development process an issue largely in the technical order. We have to plan the kind of society we are developing into if we are to have development at all.

[26]Kenneth Boulding, "The Economics of Spaceship Earth," in *Collected Papers*, vol. 2 (Boulder: University of Colorado Press, 1971), p. 389.

Finally, the concept of spaceship economics has given us back our membership in the human species and has made our situation again part of the human career. Spaceship economics has to be thought of as a planetary system, a system for which we lack precedent, rules, or adequate institutions, but must nevertheless learn to deal with.

So it seems that we shall now ask again, How can some moral order control our technical order, and what kind of moral order will that be? And what kind of moral order can our technical order create for us to live in? Economic development will again be seen as part of the human career on earth.

Chapter 4 / SOCIAL PLANNING
The Attempt to Enter the Moral
Order via the Technical Order

One way, it might be supposed, that the technical order might be integrated with the moral order, and the moral order itself taken in hand, in the interests of rational command over social development and avoidance of social problems, is through the development of the field in planning known as "social planning." The concept of social planning is, by now, no longer a novelty, although it currently is used to designate more than one kind of activity. John Dyckman, in a paper on the topic,[1] distinguishes three general meanings of the term:

[1]John Dyckman, "Social Planning, Social Planners and Planned Societies," *Journal of the American Institute of Planners* 32, no. 2 (1966): 67–68.

(1) societal planning, (2) the programming for selected social goals, and (3) deliberate introduction of social values into economic and political processes. Dyckman says that social planning in the United States generally means the second category, dealing with specific social programs made necessary for repairing the damage done by prior programs of public intervention, such as relocation programs associated with urban renewal. In what is sometimes referred to as "the international field" or "development planning," the focus on social programs is not quite so clearly dominant. It may well be that in practice most social planning consists of programming in such sectors as health, education, and housing, but at some levels of discussion Dyckman's third category is very generously represented.

The Social Planning Section of the Social Development Division of the United Nations developed (in 1970) a "Correspondence Training Program in Social Planning" that is intended to help in developing "a new type of planner, a social planner." The social planner is described as one

> who can assist in identifying the social prerequisites of development and the social impediments to development and in anticipating the social cost of development; who will focus attention on these factors in formulating plans and in designing machinery for their implementation and who will attempt to include in the policy ambit considerations relating to participation of the population in development—participation both in its benefits and in the planning for it.[2]

What exactly is the nature of this activity of social planning? It should be noted at the outset that the definition

---

[2]United Nations, "Introductory Note," *Correspondence Training Program in Social Planning* (1970) p. 3.

provided by the United Nations syllabus includes, as only one aspect, the programming of "social programs," as in health and in education, which Dyckman saw were the center of social planning in the United States. The syllabus offered by the United Nations makes a sweep a good deal wider than that and, in the process, presents a significant number of interesting ambiguities that the authors freely state in their introduction:

1. The interest of the United Nations in the field of activity which later came to be termed social planning may be traced back to the early 1950's. At this time, questions relating to the inter-dependence between the economic and social aspects of development and of the consequent need to integrate social and economic action in long-term planning assumed importance in the discussion of the inter-governmental bodies.

2. While discussions in the United States in the subsequent years implied what was meant by social planning, no attempt was made to define the term explicitly. It was clear, however, that the main area of concern was with planning for balanced and/or integrated social and economic development (of the developing countries) and that broadly defined social planning was concerned with social aspects closely related to economic development and which lay outside the scope of conventional planning. Inter-relationships was therefore a central concept: inter-relationships among social sectors (education, health, housing, social welfare, etc.) and between social sectors and economic sectors.

3. In later years concern regarding the failure of many development plans signified the need for re-thinking the planning process and identified many social factors requiring attention. These were also concerned with the omission from the

planning system of matters relating to the distribution within the nation of the benefits of growth.

4. As the United Nations course approach to social planning has evolved it has focused on the improvement of levels of living, the avoidance of social costs (adverse consequence of development), the social requirements for growth, the obstacles to planned development and lastly on the distribution of the benefits of growth. No universally accepted unified doctrine and organizational structure for social planning has yet emerged however.[3]

This statement, in consonance with the UN course as a whole, frankly exhibits the interesting ambiguity of the social-planning or social-planner role, and raises, indeed, the question as to the degree to which social planning is to be performed by social planners. Broadly defined, social planning has a large-scale mandate, touching on the ends and the means of development. At the same time, the materials of the course suggest the unclear mandate of the social planner; his lack of any clear position is the institutional structure, and the way in which his search for identity and for institutional base is dominated by the preeminence of the economists in the field of development planning.

If one takes a fairly conventional definition of planning, for example, A. Waterston's, quoted in the UN materials as "an organized intelligent attempt to select the best available alternatives to achieve specific goals,"[4] it becomes clear that social factors, social research, and social planning can appear

[3]*Ibid.*, p. 1.
[4]Albert Waterston, *Development Planning: Lessons of Experience* (Baltimore: The Johns Hopkins Press, 1965), p. 8.

at a number of points. The term "organized" suggests problems of institutional functioning and institutional change, for some time a developed field in the behavioral sciences, and an area in which applied research might well contribute to the planning of development programs and of the planning activity itself. "Intelligent" suggests problems of research and information input, and the strategic use of various kinds of social research, social indicators, and the like. "Best" suggests study of the values held by various groups in the society, and policy-focused studies of who gains and who loses and what is gained and lost by alternative strategies and programs. "Available" suggests studies of political and institutional feasibility. "Goals" suggests the delineation of specific social-welfare targets, and, beyond that, perhaps alternative views of the good and alternative models of society.

The idea of social planning, however, does not spring up simply from such considerations, but clearly has developed as a counterbalance to economic planning. Development planning as a formal activity, although not necessarily in all cases the modernization process itself, has been dominated by the methodology of economics and the instrumentalities of economic inputs and economic institutions. In all discussions of social planning above the level of programming for selected social goals, it is clear that the field has come into existence as an input to the area of action traditionally dominated by economists.

A certain demand for additional or modifying input into the planning process has been generated by a common sense that conventional economic planning overlooks a number of critical issues, both of means and of consequences. As the UN documents point out

> The Expert Group on Social Policy and Planning held at Stockholm from 1–10 September 1969 considered that

> the emphasis on accelerating growth of national income in the preparations for the Second Development Decade neglected many of the critical problems of developing countries such as the dualist social structure, inequalities, unemployment and development of human potential. The fact that development either leaves behind, or in some ways even creates large areas of poverty, stagnation, marginality and actual exclusion from economic and social progress was felt by the Group to require urgent consideration of development strategy.[5]

It has become evident that regional and class inequalities are not self-correcting in the development process, but may even become greater. The "culture of poverty" is described by Oscar Lewis as a condition of developing, rather than of traditional, societies. On the other hand, examples are not lacking of attempts to implement economic-development programs which have fallen victim to cultural and institutional barriers. (The UN course tactfully omits citations, but one might think, for example, of Kusum Nair's *Blossoms in the Dust*,[6] or such case studies as Amuzegar's *Technical Assistance in Theory and Practice: The Case of Iran*.

Thus, a certain intellectual market had opened up, as one might say, for social planners, or social planning, or, at least, for some sort of modification of the development-planning process which would incorporate consideration of social factors in development. What modifications should these be? In what manner should the social factors be taken into account in development planning? In respect to these questions, the UN documents are frank and interesting in sketching out various schemes.

---

[5]United Nations, "Introduction to Social Planning," in *Correspondence Training*.
[6]Kusum Nair, *Blossoms in the Dust: The Human Factor in Indian Development* (New York: Frederick A. Praeger, 1961). Jahangir Amuzegar, *Technical Assistance in Theory and Practice: The Case of Iran* (New York: Praeger, 1966).

One approach is that identified by Donald V. Mc-Granahan as "Social Planning as Planning for Minimum Levels of Adequacy":

> The purpose of development planning is to achieve maximum possible economic growth while at the same time ensuring minimum social levels—minimum shelter, minimum health care, minimum education, etc. The establishment of these minimum levels of adequacy (which will change with economic development), and decisions regarding the most appropriate means of achieving them, would constitute social planning under this conception. However, social factors contributing to economic development would also be taken into account, in planning for the fastest possible economic growth.[7]

From the point of view of the claims of social planning, this definition of the situation may be regarded as a minimum position, allowing social goals to be satisfied and social factors to be recognized only when all other claims are satisfied. Indeed it seems to derive from the view that there is a basic conflict between the capital accumulation necessary for development and present consumption, which leads the development planner to try to keep expenditures on welfare and other consumption down to the least possible. As a position from which social planning might proceed, it suffers not only from making minimal impact as defined but also from certain difficulties of longer-term strategy. This way of thinking of the problem is bound to make social programs an extra cost, since the social consequences are not taken into account in developing the economic strategy. Sectorial planning of social programs can never provide the sort of input that might, for example, try to handle the social-welfare issues through de-

---

[7]"Approaches to Social Planning," in United Nations, *Correspondence Training.*

veloping the sort of economic institutions that channel investment from the lower-income sectors (for instance, through urban policies that make land available to the poor or through new techniques and new marketing institutions in agriculture), and thus allow these sectors a larger share of the economic pie.

To separate planning of economic growth from planning for welfare, and to institute special programs for dealing with the welfare issue, is likely to be a very expensive way of proceeding, except for those governments so able to disregard the claims for welfare that, in all probability, nothing more sophisticated than a few charitable enterprises is required.

This version of social planning as "planning for minimum levels of adequacy" casts the social planner as the recipient of those crumbs that fall from the budgetary table presided over by economists. It was thus only natural that social planners should seize eagerly at a different formulation of the problem, which appeared to guarantee them a regular seat at the central planning budget. Such a formula appeared to be provided by the discovery of "investment in human capital" as an intrinsic part of the development-planning process.

In this view of things, investment in health and education no longer appears as part of a welfare policy, but rather as a sound dollars-and-cents investment in productivity, and, indeed, in some developed versions of the argument, among the most productive forms of investment possible. It is even possible, under this trend of events, to separate social planning from social-welfare planning, as proposed in UN course material:

> The social welfare planner is viewed as attached to the Ministry of Social Welfare, whereas the social planner is working side by side with economic planners within the central planning agency. The social planner is gen-

erally concerned with both the social factors and the
social goals of development, although he is not attached
to any social sector in particular. The social welfare planner is helping the Ministry of Social Welfare prepare his
own share or sector of the national plan.[8]

However, this position turns out in practice to be more
slippery than it might appear at first glance. Even if one as-
sumes, not unreasonably, that investments in education,
health, and housing all contribute to productivity, just how
much does a unit of input contribute? And how do you know
when it is more productive to invest in education as against
nutrition, and when the reverse is the case? Even if one has
measures of cost-effectiveness for each sector, one cannot
necessarily compare across sectors. How are planners to
measure output in any case? A case in point is that of the
current struggles over accountability in education in the
United States, in the course of which it has become clear that
it is very difficult indeed to connect specific input expenditures with measurable outputs of education. Furthermore, it
is coming to be recognized that there is no reason to believe
that the most efficient form of educational input for all times
and places is schools at all, and if educational investment in
human capital is now seen to include newspapers, radio, on-
the-job training, and community organization, the problem
of measurement becomes elusive.

Most distressing of all for the social planners who adopt
this ploy is to find themselves boxed by their own rhetoric
into the need for justifying their programs on the basis of
their economic payoff, and thus, in effect, confirming the
economists in their domination of planning.

A series of economic studies indicating that a very large

[8]"Social Welfare Planning," *ibid*.

share in the generation of economic growth must be attributed to an ill-defined but largely "social" residual factor rather than to input of capital and labor, induced economic planners to turn their attention to this aspect. At the same time, speculations began to be heard on the possibility of constructing mathematical models incorporating all of the social as well as the economic variables relevant to development. This support was received by the promoters of the social programs with gratification mixed with a certain uneasiness. They could not accept the investment criterion as primary without risking, from the human rights point of view, serious distortions in the content of the social programs and a refusal to allocate any resources to forms of social action for which "returns" could not be demonstrated. At the same time, the initial attempts to measure returns on investment in such sectors as education and health or to treat these sectors as input–output models led to such formidable conceptual and practical difficulties that some economists have come to doubt whether such exercises will ever be useful tools in the quest for criteria for social allocations.[9]

Another tack which could be taken to avoid this set of dilemmas was to argue the value of social planning to reduce the "social costs" of development:

Social planning is concerned with minimizing the social costs of economic growth and social change, and with anticipating social problems which are likely to arise in different development situations. Industrial and agricultural development may involve social costs which are rarely taken into account in estimating the returns of the project. For example, in some cases large scale irrigation schemes have led to an increased incidence of bilharziasis . . . with negative results on productivity, family

[9]"Social Development and Social Policy," *ibid.*

levels of living, etc. . . . The establishment of a new industrial complex may cause air and water pollution
. . . and social costs in terms of private and public ex-
penditure on health care and recreation, together with
non-monetary social costs to individuals resulting from
loss of recreation facilities, increased morbidity, etc.[10]

That such social costs exist, and that they should be taken
into account, is incontrovertible. But, here again, there are
inherent difficulties. Agreement as to the reality of the problem hardly seems to offer a clear channel of action or a clear
institutional base for the social planner. Social costs are at
least as hard to compute as social benefits, and equally difficult to integrate neatly into development planning as conventionally practiced. How do you compute the costs of a
dam to people who must be evacuated elsewhere in its building? How do you compare these costs with the benefits to
them and to others now and in the future? Furthermore, how
are we to imagine the role of the social planner as social cost
reckoner? It seems likely that the social-planner role here becomes the unwelcome one of project critic, and although we
may easily recognize this role as one with which we have had
experience, we recognize by the same token that the role is
one which rapidly wears out its welcome within the planning
institution.

Still another possible view is to treat social planning as
dealing with means, with the implementation of development
programs. Social planning in this area has a substantial research base in the study of social and economic change, of
institutional innovation, and of the relationship of government institutions to their clients and to their fields of action.
Active practice in this spectrum, however, seems to reside

[10]"Introduction to Social Planning," *ibid.*, p. 12.

mainly in the field of community organization and community-action programs. In itself this contrast seems to provide a clue to the characteristic difficulties of the social planner as dealing with implementation. Implementation is embedded in political-social processes, and deals with, if it does not actually collide with, important vested interests. Thus, as a *practice* this kind of approach will tend to be kept to the lower level of things, outside the central planning–national development strategy level. The history of the community-action programs generated as part of the War on Poverty in the United States provides a suggestive example of the tension between institutional innovation at the grass roots level and institutional interests at a higher level.

A final version of the task of social planning sees it as dealing with goals. Under the title "Levels of Living and Social Objectives," the United Nations course provides material dealing with the methodology for constructing a "level of living index which would provide a social counterpart to GNP,"[11] together with some comments on the relationship between social objectives and targets in developing planning. The comment is made that the idea of social goals and social targets is much more firmly established in some areas than in others: education, health, "and to a less extent housing" tend to be developed in this way. On the other hand, although "many plans explicitly state that another major purpose of development is a more equitable distribution of income and the level of living . . . among the plans reviewed none was found to contain a comprehensive and systematic policy to effect a better distribution."[12]

In this respect, the comment of John Saul seems apposite:

[11]"Levels of Living and Social Objectives," *ibid.*, p. 7.
[12]*Ibid.*, p. 21.

It is, no doubt, unfortunate that, in order for these issues (of class equality) to be adequately represented at the highest levels of power, there cannot be, say, a Ministry for the Avoidance or Mitigation of Class Formation, yet this difficulty is inherent in the issue itself. For class formation is the product of a number of processes—cultural, economic, social, political—and cannot be readily compartmentalized; it is thus the problem of all ministries. The danger, of course, is that the responsibility of all becomes the task of none and this has tended to be the case in more than one "socialist" country.[13]

Some may actually argue that the "social goals" are the true ends of development, the economic targets merely means. This view, also, receives its expression in the documents provided by the UN, although only in a minor way:

While social factors can be viewed as contributing to economic production goals, the opposite approach is also conceivable in planning. According to this more radical approach, the social values which by common agreement are the final goals of economic development should, in fact, be treated as such in the planning model. The economic production of goods and services should be dealt with in the plan as a means, along with various other means to social ends, and not, in effect, as the end. Economic planning in this conception becomes subordinated to a broadly conceived social planning. Individual economic projects are evaluated primarily in terms of their social contributions, present and future, which would include, however, their capacity to generate future income for future social benefits, and would also include consideration of certain undesirable consequences of economic projects.

[13]John V. Saul, "High Level Manpower for Socialism, "in Idrian N. Resnick (ed.), *Tanzania: Revolution by Education* (Arusha, Tanzania: Longmans of Tanzania, 1968), p. 95.

The formulation of a national planning model in which
social values are incorporated as final aims raises in turn
a number of technical questions, which are generally no
more difficult than those raised by the human resources
approach discussed above. There is, however, the additional problem, as discussed above, of determining the
optimum pattern of social objectives and the optimum
distribution of social benefits across time and across
space.

This approach to social planning is still in a preliminary
stage of investigation and experimentation.[14]

Since this version of social planning is evidently one that
lays the broadest claims on the development process, one
might suppose that, in the best tradition of professional ag-
grandizement, this definition of the problem would be one
frequently put forward by social planners. It is not.

In this view of social planning, the difficulty of treating
planning as a technical activity is much too exposed for comfort. When one gets to this point with social planning, one
is clearly in political life in the very broadest sense. Indeed,
if one were to look for representation of this view, I think that
one would find it, not in the area of planning, but in the
rhetoric of politics at the national level, where, to be sure, it
tends to make up in grandeur what it lacks in specificity.

In contrast, planning may be said to succeed as an activity
because it is a style of dealing with the problems of human
life in societies in a technical manner—a manner that lacks
grandeur and that deals with problems with a good deal more
information and somewhat more rationality than might be
the case if they were treated within the conventions of regular
political life. It might be argued that economic planning has

[14]McGranahan, "Approaches," pp. 6–7.

as much power as it has not only because of the power of economic incentives and disincentives to shape the lives of men, but because the forms of economic analysis have a particular neatness and clarity—deceptive, of course, and we know it, but we need it and use it still—in their handling of problems of choice and of values. Yet we know that our communal life, including our economic institutions, cannot be thought of wholly in technical terms, and at the same time we know that we must apply technical criteria to it. The idea of social planning is one way in which we try to deal with the ambiguities of the situation. No wonder, then, that social planning itself proves ambiguous, a concept that inevitably becomes self-contradictory.

In 1917, the sociologist Robert Park asked to comment on the relevance of the war to sociology, attempted to confront these contradictions when he commented instead on the relevance of the war to the forms of society and, thus, to social theory:

> The traditional division of the social sciences is inherited from a period when the dominant English political theory was individualism; when the state was regarded as a sort of umpire whose function was to preserve the peace between mutually competing and antagonistic individuals; when the government that governed least was the government that governed best, and social welfare was achieved when the natural harmony of antagonistic interests was maintained.

> With the rise of the industrial state, organized politically and economically for international competition and international war, the scene changes. The exigencies of the new situation demand of the state not merely freedom, but efficiency. The radicals want not merely individual liberty, but social justice. These demands conflict and the reconciliation is at once an economic and a political problem. It is a nest of problems.

> After this war we shall perhaps no longer think of social
> problems as exclusively economic, political, or social-
> welfare problems. These will rather represent aspects,
> points of view, from which almost any social problem
> may be viewed. It will be easier perhaps to think of them
> as: administrative problems, i.e., problems of efficiency;
> problems of social politics and public policy, i.e., legis-
> lative problems; or finally, problems of social forces,
> tendencies, trends.[15]

We still do not have an adequate language for discussing
this "nest of problems," or for dealing with social forms that
are understood to be politically expressive and technically
effective, in order to meet the demands for both liberty and
social justice. The lack of such a language is one basic reason
for the ambiguity of social planning.

In the meantime, it might be useful to think of social
planning as a range of activities that in various ways aims at
creating a more effective politics—not in the sense of achieving specifically political ends, but in the sense implied in the
quotation of achieving a society that is better, in a sense both
instrumental and moral. Because the social forms with which
it deals are to be thought of as having political and instrumental aspects, it is important to think of them as evolving
through a process that is political and technical, involving
information and analysis. We may think of this process as
one of developing an issue-oriented politics, or as one of
developing a politically based and politically operational
planning.

In such a view, political devices like decentralization and
citizen participation and advocacy are to be seen as lying at
one end of a continuum occupied at the other by such research

[15]Robert E. Park, "Sociology and the War," *American Journal of Sociology*, 23
(July, 1917): 64.

techniques as social indicators, opinion surveys, program-evaluation research, and community studies. We must understand that all these research and planning activities are part of our political life, broadly understood; and we must understand also that our political institutions are channels not only of power but also of information as to what people want, what they will stand for, and what and for whom the consequences of policy are.

The Cuban experiment discussed in Chapter 5 shows us what full-blown societal planning is all about. A look at such a system suggests why societal planning is not a job for planners; at least, if these are defined as technicians. Where, as in Cuba, the technical and the political are completely intertwined, it is almost impossible to separate a realm of the technical. Such a system raises all the issues of power and consensus that a complex industrial society like the United States can manage in part to finesse by dividing the realm of decision between politics and the market, and by confining social planning to specific realms of program development.

Chapter 5 / MORAL INCENTIVES IN CUBA
The Politicizing of Work

In primitive societies, the technical order becomes embedded in the moral order through a kind of implicit, unformalized, trial-and-error evolution of customary behavior within what is bound to be, after all, a relatively small local group. In a modern society, this requires what has been referred to in the preceding chapter as *societal planning*.

I shall explore the implications of societal planning by looking at an instance of it—the transformation of Cuba in the course of the Revolution. The exploration will focus on work, because work, a central institution in the technical order of economic production, is also central to the social structure and to individual motivation, and is thus the central point at which the individual relates to society.

Work, in this respect, has a double aspect. It can be seen as elicited from the individual by others, through payment, force, or persuasion; it can also be seen as a form of self-expression. In the first aspect, it is the cost of life; expelled from Eden, Adam was cursed by having to earn his living by the sweat of his brow. We pay for work; what we do by choice, unpaid, is our avocation. Societies build systems of incentives, both positive rewards and negative sanctions, so that work will get done. But in the second aspect, work has also been seen as a man's "calling," his craft, his means of self-expression, his way of joining with his fellows in some common purpose. Freud saw the fully functioning human being as able to work and to love—and the two were, in his thought, not entirely unconnected expressions of the same basic life-force.

Human work is also, necessarily, coordinated, and as we have developed more complex and articulated systems of technology and wider and more complex systems of exchange it has become more intricately coordinated. The systems by which work is coordinated are also systems of power and prestige. These systems are basic to social organization, as well as to the systems of sentiment that articulate men's conduct as individual members of societies. The subject of work is not merely economic; it is also social and political, in the broad sense. These aspects can be treated separately; they can also be joined.

Anthropologists have been at pains to show how, in primitive societies, the activities of production and distribution are not treated as a sphere separate from the rest. Trade appears first as a specialized sort of transaction involving strangers; the distribution of food and other goods in the primitive community is an aspect of the organization of society, structured through kinship and other social ties. So, too, the organization of work emerges out of and rests on a body of understanding more social and cultural in character than "economic," in the special sense in which we now use the word.[1]

In an essay some years ago, Gerard Piel wrote that

> property and work are artifacts of civilization. In the kinship economies of pre-agricultural societies they have no place whatever or appear only in the faintest analogues. . . . Hunting and food-gathering are not work but adventure, assertion of manhood, magic and craft.
>
> Property and work make their appearance with the agricultural revolution. . . . They are devices for gathering and impounding the surplus that four families at work upon the land can now produce to support a fifth family off the land. Property is the institution by which the church, the state, and their individual agents assert their control over the other primary factor of production—the energy of human muscle. The word "work" signifies toil and at the same time the product of toil; it is the measure ("according to his works") of the portion of the product that may be allocated to the unpropertied worker.[2]

With that great social transformation which we call the Industrial Revolution a dramatically new mode and a new theory of social organization came about: the *market*.[3] In social theory, and to a substantial degree in practice, work became a commodity to be offered, demanded, and remunerated ac-

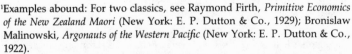

[1]Examples abound: For two classics, see Raymond Firth, *Primitive Economics of the New Zealand Maori* (New York: E. P. Dutton & Co., 1929); Bronislaw Malinowski, *Argonauts of the Western Pacific* (New York: E. P. Dutton & Co., 1922).

[2]*Consumers of Abundance* (Santa Barbara, Calif.: Center for the Study of Democratic Institutions, 1961).

[3]Karl Polanyi, *The Great Transformation* (Toronto: Farrar & Rinehart, 1944).

cording to the laws of supply and demand. Of all the painful aspects of the transformation, perhaps this was felt most acutely. It took many years of worker organization to alter the situation in which "freeborn men felt that to go voluntarily into a factory was to surrender their birthright, which a Leveller had defined as property in one's own person and labor," and in which peasants saw day labor as "a kind of hell into which peasants may fall if things are not bettered."[4]

Yet, in a sense, we have to recognize that the conception of the market is a partial model of a system having many other aspects. As the relatively simple industrial enterprises of Marx's time have given way to more complex and elaborately organized ones, with elaborate wage-differentiated hierarchies and specializations, and as unions have taken a larger and larger part in the determination of wages, labor has become, if a commodity, at least less and less a commodity "like any other." Wages have clearly a sociology and a politics, and the organization of work and the rewards of work have other than simply technical or market determinants.[5]

Nor could it be said that economic activity is called forth simply by monetary incentives. Housework is the clearest— and largest—example of a whole body of labor in modern industrial societies that still functions outside the economic market-transaction model, but many other sorts of work, even in such societies, rely substantially on other than market incentives. Although the mercenary army is a recognized institution, since the Napoleonic era no modern nation has yet fought a major war on market incentives alone.

[4]Christopher Hill, *Reformation to Industrial Revolution* (Harmondsworth, Middlesex, England: Penguin Books, 1969), p. 262.
[5]Barbara Wootton, *The Social Foundations of Wage Policy: A Study of Contemporary British Wage and Salary Structure* (London: Allen & Unwin, 1955).

What we like to think of as a system of "material incentives" for work turns out, on inspection, to be not so clearly material after all.

> Pay is simply a shared symbolic way of recognizing accomplishment in our society. Thus if pay does not represent accomplishment, it loses much of its ability to satisfy such needs as esteem and recognition, and thus loses much of its importance.[6]

Furthermore, no modern government is prepared to allow market transactions free scope to shape the form of society or the conditions of life for its participants. As human societies have become more technologically advanced and more interdependent, as economic institutions have become ever larger and more powerful, the role of political institutions in coordinating these institutions, in providing them with the conditions for growth, and in regulating their effects for other than strictly "economic ends" has become more, rather than less, important.[7] As for developing countries, it is hard now to conceive of the idea of such a process going on in the absence of some sort of national planning and a substantial amount of government leadership and government intervention, under the umbrella of some sort of nationalist ideology.

Development always has both political means and political ends. It has remained, however, for the Chinese and the Cubans to propose an image of development in which the process and the institutions of economic growth are treated frankly as central forces in the political process, as the way of creating a new sort of more egalitarian society and a new

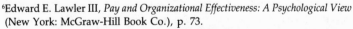

[6]Edward E. Lawler III, *Pay and Organizational Effectiveness: A Psychological View* (New York: McGraw-Hill Book Co.), p. 73.
[7]See John Kenneth Galbraith, *The New Industrial State* (Boston: Houghton Mifflin Co., 1971).

sort of citizen. They have had no less a commitment to growth than any other country,[8] but they set out to bring about growth in such a way as to transform society in the most fundamental way. In this process, the institutions of work, and the meaning of work, have been central.

Of these two cases, I shall examine the Cuban attempt to carry out economic development on the basis of "moral incentives." It is an experiment still in progress; the version developed after 1970 was no longer the same as that I was able to observe in 1968, for the failure of the goals set for the sugar harvest in that year set the leadership of the Revolution to reevaluate its methods, and to move simultaneously toward a greater use of material incentives and the decentralizing of political participation. But in looking at the experiment, I shall focus mainly on its appearance in 1968 at the time of my visit: this would now appear something of a high point of its history. There is full and interesting literature on this experiment, as to its relationship to Marxist economic theory and as to its outcome in economic practice. I shall rely on some of this work[9] without, certainly doing it justice here, as well

[8]For the centrality of productivity in Mao's model of development with politics taking command, see J. Gray, "The Economics of Maoism," *Bulletin of the Atomic Scientists,* 25, no. 2 (1969): 196; reprinted in *Underdevelopment and Development: The Third World Today,* ed. Henry Bernstein (Harmondsworth: Penguin, 1973).

[9]Especially, Robert M. Bernardo, *The Theory of Moral Incentives in Cuba* (Tuscaloosa: University of Alabama Press, 1971); Bertram Silverman, *Man and Socialism in Cuba: The Great Debate* (New York: Atheneum, 1971); *idem,* "Economic Organization and Social Conscience: Some Dilemmas of Cuban Socialism," in *Cuba: The Logic of the Revolution,* ed. David Barkin and Nita R. Manitzas (Andover, Mass.:Warner Modular Publications, 1973); C. Mesa-Lago, "Cuba: Teoría y práctica de los incentivos," *Aportes,* 20 (April 1971): 70–112; "Ideological, Political and Economic Factors in the Cuban Controversy on Material versus Moral Incentives," *Journal of Inter-American Studies and World Affairs,* 14, no. 1 (February 1972): 49–106; David Barkin, "Popular

as on my own observations of the Cuban way of economic development when I visited there in 1968 for just under a month.

When our small group arrived in Cuba, we were just in time for the annual 26th of July gathering at which the major speech (delivered, of course, by Fidel Castro) focused on the peculiar character of the Cuban development model:

> And we should not use money or wealth to create political awareness. We must use political awareness to create wealth. To offer a man more to do more than his duty is to buy his conscience with money. To give a man participation in more collective wealth because he does his duty and produces more for society is to turn political awareness into wealth.
>
> As we said before, communism certainly cannot be established if we do not create abundant wealth. But the way to do this, in our opinion, is not by creating wealth with money or with wealth, but by creating wealth with political awareness and more and more collective wealth with more collective political awareness.
>
> The road is not easy.[10]

Hearing these words, it seemed to me that Castro was turning Marxist theory back on itself: the superstructure, the system of ideas, was to order and transform the economic structure. As an American socialist later commented: "The anomaly is that Cuban leaders. . .have in effect spiritualized problems of economic production and allocation."[11]

Moreover, I perceived that the speech was not simply

Participation and the Dialectics of Cuban Development" and Terry Karl, "Work Incentives in Cuba," in *Latin American Perspectives*, issue 7, supplement 1975, vol. II, no. 4.

[10]Fidel Castro, speech of July 26, 1968, in *Granma* (July 28, 1968): 5.

[11]Irving Louis Horwitz, "Introduction" to Bernardo, *Theory of Moral Incentives*, p. xviii.

stating these ideas, that it was a social event in which the
ideas, the model of development, were themselves embodied.
Our group sat on bleachers that were placed around a huge
stadium lined with billboards exhorting "giving"—Giving
sweat, Giving blood. The bleachers were full of people, and
the stadium, too, was jammed with more thousands of people—perhaps a half million—who moved continually, and
who were addressed by the speaker directly, and who in turn,
shouted back. Castro's speeches are expository: popular lec-
tures. But the crowd in the stadium was not just a lecture
audience. They were also pilgrims. Many had travelled
through the night to reach the stadium on time. Our group
had driven in the dark along roads clotted with people, some
on foot, some in cars, some standing, often singing, in the
open stake-trucks used to transport sugar cane. The event in
the stadium was the annual festival of the faith. My friends
and I had come to Cuba as to a sort of land of fable; it seemed
to me that what I was experiencing was even more extraordinary than what I had expected.

Previous to this event, and this statement and enactment
of the Cuban path to development, there lay already in 1968
fifteen years of Castro's movement since the abortive assault
on the Moncada barracks, and nearly a decade of experience
as guerrilla fighters in power. Back of it also was a great deal
of remarkably open and articulate discussion, in particular
that discussion among Cuban leadership spanning the years
from 1962 to 1965 and usually referred to as "the Great Debate" over the appropriate forms of economic organization
and incentives for socialist society in transition. The Great
Debate, in which the advocates of revolutionary ethics confronted the "economist" supporters of more conventional
economic rationality, was concerned with the appropriate
organizational forms for a socialist planned economy, with

the incentives for managerial and worker effort, with the role of ideas in respect to economic forms and forces, and, by implication, with the meaning of economic activity in a socialist society in process.

When the leaders of the 26th of July Movement came to power, they came as men without a very clearly articulated theoretical model of action. The leaders of the Revolution were clearly Marxist—Castro himself a "Utopian Marxist," he said, since his last years as a university student—but the movement itself seems to have been in character more nationalist and social reformist. The 1953 program of the movement for "an efficient and honest government which by its actions will stimulate, protect, finance, combat or supply private business and make all of us more prosperous"[12] suggested a good deal of central planning and state entrepreneurship, a fairly high rate of economic growth, and greater social equality, but nothing of the new society and New Man which were by 1968 to constitute the objectives of the Revolution.

Nationalism, social reform, and economic development were joined as naturally connected goals by Cuban history, for the foreign domination that had repeatedly permitted the United States to arrange the Cuban political system for its own ends was also the bulwark of an economic system that made Cuba an economic appendage of the United States and, in so doing, maintained an internal structure on the island displaying underutilized resources, gross inequalities in income, and minimal growth rate. While the giant sugar producers held vast tracts of land idle, Cuba imported about $200 million of agricultural commodities a year. Unemployment

[12]Theses of the Revolutionary Movement of July 26.

even during the sugar harvest came to around 9% of the labor force, and during the months of the "dead season" between harvests at least a fifth of Cuban workers were unemployed. Although a quarter of the population was illiterate, thousands of teachers could not find jobs. Cuba bought 80% of her imports from the United States, and the country was a net exporter of capital; an American economist, talking with some Cuban radicals in Brazil a few years before the Revolution, asked them what they would do on taking power. "Oh," they laughed, "I guess we'll have to invade the southern United States to reclaim our investments in land"[13]—for the earnings of the Cuban economy had been going northward.

In this situation, when the guerrillas took power, there seemed to be no need for making choices or for strategic discussions; everything was to be done, and it appeared as if, with the slack in the economy left by the departure of the Americans, anything could be. The first years of "free wheeling"[14] did not generate policy discussion so much as ad hoc programming, centering around the process of taking command of the Cuban economy, which, piece by piece, came under the command of the new revolutionary state—directed, one must remember, not by technocrats but by men with little or no economic or managerial background, whose most recent work experience had been that of guerrilla fighters.

The original economic strategy of industrializing on the basis of an expanded and diversified agriculture proved more difficult than had been foreseen, and had to be abandoned for a return to the "tyranny" of the sugar monoculture; shortages developed and rationing had to be introduced; it was

[13]Conversation reported to me by Alex Ganz.
[14]See Edward Boorstein, *The Economic Transformation of Cuba: A First Hand Account* (New York: Monthly Review Press, 1968).

clear that economic coordination had broken down. A number of experts from the European socialist countries came to Cuba to help in the formulation of the first economic plan in 1962. Out of this context came the "Great Debate" in which most of the members of the Council of Ministers participated, and a number of foreign Marxists as well.

All the participants in the debate agreed on the Marxist principle that institutions and goals must conform to the realities of objective economic forces. All participants also agreed on the need for comprehensive economic planning in socialist development.

But one group, the economists, particularly concerned with the inefficiency which they saw in administered free-wheeling, saw the remedy as lying in a greater attention to costs, in decentralization, and in the provision of material incentives for workers and for managers that would make them responsible for greater efficiency. They argued that, so long as the productive apparatus was unable to provide goods in such quantity as to guarantee to each "according to his needs," no change in legal ownership could do away with the stage of commodity production. Furthermore, they thought that the centralized administration of the economy was beyond the technical capacity of the overworked revolutionary government. During a substantial transitional period, they expected the various economic enterprises should trade with each other, borrow credit, strive for profitability, and respond to economic stimuli, always subject, of course, to central planning and control. This strategy, they thought, would produce greater efficiency in the short run and would be, in this way, the most efficient path to that period of plenty in the long run in which Cuba might at last distribute its reward on the basis of "from each according to his ability; to each according to his needs."

The leader of the competing point of view was Che Guevara, who even in 1960 had rather astonished the French expert René Dumont with his views on the role of consciousness in the development process. Dumont had visited Guevara—"the man most responsible for Cuban economic policy"—to persuade him that the current policies of a very centralized management of agriculture were leading to irresponsibility by lower-level management and by workers, and that what was needed was a system of producers' cooperatives from which could come *"a sense of co-ownership*, and a personal attachment to their work collective." To this notion, Dumont tells us, "Che reacted violently: 'You have put too much emphasis on the sense of ownership' " and he went on to outline

> a position that was very interesting in principle, a sort of ideal vision of Socialist Man, who would become a stranger to the mercantile side of things, working for society and not for profit. He was very critical of the industrial success of the Soviet Union, where, he said, everybody works and strives and tries to go beyond his quota, but only to earn more money. He did not think the Soviet Man was really a new sort of man, for he did not find him any different, really from a Yankee. He refused to consciously participate in the creation in Cuba of a second American society, even if everything belongs to the State.[15]

Guevara, who took part in the Great Debate both through a number of theoretical articles in Cuban journals and through his own policies as the powerful director of the industrial sector of the Cuban economy, believed that a mode of development more centralized, more administered, and less

[15]René Dumont, *Cuba: Socialism and Development* (New York: Grove Press, 1970), pp. 51–52.

materialistic than that proposed by the economists was not only desirable but quite possible for Cuba. He believed that, given the small size of the Cuban economy and modern techniques of planning and programming—on which he placed a great deal and perhaps an inordinate degree of confidence—state ownership would make possible an administered economy in which men could learn, through an educational process directed by the revolutionary government, to choose socially needed tasks and to strive for socially valuable goals out of conscience, not for material reward.

The issue of moral versus material incentives as it appeared in the Great Debate was closely tied to issues of administrative centralization versus decentralization. Guevara stood strongly for the policy of central planning and centralized economic control: the economists for a system of "self-finance" in which managers of each enterprise would, while having as their primary goal fulfillment of the plan, be required to cover the enterprise's current costs with its own revenues and to ensure the profitability of production.

The proponents of this model believed that central planners could never have information complete enough to allocate resources efficiently through all parts of the system; it is probably not chance that advocates of "autofinance" were strongest in the agricultural sector of the economy, for, as one Cuban planner explained to us, "planning in agriculture is different from in industry; there are always so many unforeseen events and decisions which have to be made on the spot." The proponents of autofinance believed that the provision of some administrative autonomy and the partial use of money within the productive sector would make it possible for each set of managers to determine the proper outputs and inputs from the center for maximum efficiency.

Although moral incentives may be seen as in some sense

a means to administrative decentralization—a way of getting responsible action on the part of participants in the system at the edges of a span of central control—it also appeared that, for the system of autofinance to flourish, a substantial amount of material incentives would be required.

> It would seem that to make the firm's residual goal of profit-making meaningful in the system of self-finance, the director's and worker's salary may have to be partially tied to that secondary success indicator. And the greater role of money in this system (as partial command over goods and people) would give managers greater power to use it for their purposes, which may not always coincide with centralized community values.[16]

The Great Debate also raised issues as to the role of what Marxist economists call the law of value, roughly, market profitability, in the allocation of resources in a socialist society. In the system of commodity production under capitalism, the distribution of current labor time and of the resources representing the embodied labor time of the past is achieved through each capitalist's pursuing profit by investing in industries with higher than average rate of return and disinvesting in those with a less than average. Some participants in the Great Debate argued that no change in the ownership of the productive apparatus to state control could obscure these basic allocative mechanisms and the operation of the law of value; commodity production did exist in Cuba, and planners could and should merely use these market relations more rationally.

Guevara and his supporters argued, on the contrary, that the socialization of the means of production had already so interfered with the "law of value" that mercantile relations

---

[16]Bernardo, *Theory of Moral Incentives*, pp. 31–32.

were no longer any adequate guide for allocation. For Guevara, interference with these relations was the essence of conscious planning for economic development and social justice. In any case, he argued, there could be no mercantile relationships between enterprises that were in effect all parts of one great single enterprise, the Cuban economy as owned and managed by the Cuban state; goods could be treated as commodities only as they reached the consumer or the remaining private enterprises or as they became the commodities of international trade. The allocation of resources in the Cuban economy must take place through the planning system. "The law of value and the plan are two terms linked by a contradiction and its resolution.[17]

Behind the controversy as to the role of planning in the Cuban economy lay a more general theme, which also came to enter the Debate explicitly: that of the role of ideas in transforming society. Charles Bettelheim, a French Marxist supporter of the economists, argued that

> the behavior of men—both as they relate to each other and as they function in their respective roles—should not be analyzed according to *appearances*. This would imply that altering such appearances, especially through education, would alter behavior itself; this is an idealistic outlook. Rather, behavior should be viewed as a consequence of the actual introduction of men into a given process of production and reproduction.[18]

For Guevara, in the middle of a revolution that had seized power against all apparent odds and was in the business of

---

[17]Ernesto Che Guevara, "The Meaning of Socialist Planning," in Silverman, *Man and Socialism*, p. 108.
[18]Charles Bettelheim, "On Socialist Planning and the Level and Development of the Productive Forces," in Silverman, *Man and Socialism*, pp. 32–33.

remaking society, this point of view seemed unreasonably cautious and unreasonably mechanical.

> The vanguard of the revolutionary movement, increasingly influenced by Marxist-Leninist ideology, is capable of consciously anticipating the steps to be taken in order to force the pace of events but forcing it within what is objectively possible.[19]

For Guevara, the issue of incentives was an issue as to the choice not merely of present means but of the future shape of society through the means used in the present.

> We must make it clear that *we do not deny the objective need for material incentives.* But we are unwilling to use them as primary instruments of motivation. We believe that in economics this kind of device quickly becomes a category per se and then imposes its power over man's relationships. It should be recalled that this category is a product of capitalism and is destined to die under socialism.
>
> How do we make it die?
>
> "Little by little, by means of gradually increasing the quantity of consumer goods available to the people, thereby obviating the needs for such incentives," we are told. This concept seems too mechanical, too rigid. "Consumer goods"—this is the slogan and great molder of conscience for the proponents of the other system. In our mind, however, direct material incentives and consciousness are contradictory terms.
>
> This is one point at which our differences take on meaningful dimensions. We are no longer dealing with niceties. For advocates of financial self-management, the use of direct material incentives throughout the various stages of building communism does not contradict the "development" of consciousness. But for us it does.

[19]Guevara, "The Meaning of Socialist Planning," in Silverman, *Man and Socialism*, p. 102.

It is for this reason that we struggle against the predominance of material incentives because they would retard the development of socialist morality.

If material incentives are in contradiction to the development of consciousness, but, on the other hand, a great force for obtaining production gains, should it be understood that preferential attention to the development of consciousness retards production? In comparative terms, it is possible within a given period, although no one has made the relevant calculations. We maintain that the development of consciousness does more for development of production in a relatively short time than material incentives do. . . . If in the course of experience it proves to seriously block the development of the productive forces, then the decision must be made to act quickly in order to get back on familiar paths.[20]

The statements and counter-statements that constituted the Great Debate ended in 1965, the issue not yet resolved. It is, of course, for us not yet resolved and perhaps cannot ever clearly be so. Yet we now have before us the contrasting models presented by nations that have taken, in effect, opposing positions—the nations of Eastern Europe on the one hand, and the Chinese and Cubans on the other—for in 1966 Cuba moved more radically toward a system of moral incentives, and in 1968 I found myself listening to Castro declare that

communist awareness must be developed at the same rate as the productive forces; an advance in the consciousness of revolutionaries, in the conscientiousness of the people, must accompany every step forward in the development of the productive forces. . . . We must use political awareness to create wealth.[21]

[20]Guevara, "On the Budgetary Finance System," in Silverman, *Man and Socialism*, pp. 134–5.
[21]Castro, speech of July 26, 1968, in *Granma* (July 28, 1968): 4.

The Cuban phrase "moral incentives" actually hardly does justice to the functioning of a society of this sort. It is not merely a question of prizes and penalties, but of systems of organization and motivation that encompass much more of social life and cut a good deal deeper than the term "incentives" might suggest. An Israeli sociologist, in attempting to characterize a rather similar approach to work in the early kibbutzim, uses the term "an ideology of materialistic idealism" and particularizes as follows:

> All physical and mental resources were to be harnessed and directed toward the development of a productive economy, but not for profitmaking or pleasure. The incentive to economic activity was not the prospect of material wealth and consumption but a firm commitment to a system of values. Working for the economic progress of the kibbutz thus became, to some extent, a kind of secular worship or religious service.[22]

A society organized around moral incentives can have an extraordinarily bracing tone. I found Cuba in 1968 perfectly exhilarating, putting this forth not as a judgment on the system but as data, corroborated by the many American young people who, visiting Cuba in those years, came back to the United States with a sense of dropping back into a flatter atmosphere, of coming down from a high.

For society must be organized around moral incentives just as—in the alternative model—around material ones. It can no more simply issue honors and accolades as a means of payment than another government can simply print more currency. Just as a system of currency must be redeemable

---

[22]Yonina Talmon, *Family and Community in the Kibbutz* (Cambridge: Harvard University Press, 1972), p. 206.

in material commodities, and the desirability of the material commodities supported by other social institutions (which, for example, attach prestige to driving a Cadillac), so no amount of Heroes of Moncada banners will serve as incentive unless the supporting institutions make such a moral incentive truly gratifying and desirable.

The Cubans developed a complex system of the currency of nonmaterial incentives:

> Titles vary from public praise by the leaders to medals, buttons, diplomas, plaques, certificates of communist work, and honorable mentions in factory bulletins. Other rewards include banners such as the May Day, Hundred Years of Struggle, Heroes of Moncada and Heroic Guerrilla Awards; election by the worker's peers to the mass advance-guard movement which included some 235,000 people by late May 1969; election to the even higher-ranking Communist Party; an appearance with Fidel Castro or another high official in the local Plaza de la Revolución; the yearly Hero of Labor—the highest prize to which one can aspire—and many others. And we might also include titles in a job or organization as parts of the nonmonetary incentive system; these have increased in quantity. In the 40,000-strong Youth Centennial Column which cut cane in the 1970 harvest, there were 292 brigade leaders. Some nonmonetary awards (prizes) are won individually, some collectively, examples of which were the gold medals for individuals who cut 2,500 pounds of sugarcane in the 1970 harvest and the "millionaire" brigades, respectively. Some prizes won collectively such as the Hero of Moncada banner had to be defended periodically for the right to fly it. Some prizes confer modest material benefits like vacations and pensions; but these hybrid prizes are negligible. And in the institutionalization of prizes, there are large public ceremonies several times a year in which

workers who respond to nonmonetary rewards are feted and honored for public emulation.[23]

These prizes and honors are the equivalent of the paper currency in the moral-incentive system. To make them redeemable in personal satisfaction and social approval, all the institutions of Cuban society were reorganized toward the creation of the New Man, in Castro's word's, "human beings devoid of selfishness, devoid of defects of the past, human beings with a collective sense of effort, a collective sense of strength."[24]

Although the Revolution did reduce the degree of income inequality in Cuba, partly simply through a movement to full employment and partly through somewhat more egalitarian salary scales, and although Castro declared that "the Revolution aspires—as one of the steps toward communism—to equalize incomes, from the bottom up, for all workers, regardless of the type of work they do,"[25] the viability of moral incentives in Cuba was not to be ensured through equalizing monetary incomes so much as through reducing drastically the role of monetary incomes as command over resources. Money would no longer be "a means of accumulation nor an instrument of exchange, nor a measure of value . . . stripped of its historical characteristics, it will be fundamentally a means of distribution.[26]

Rents were sharply reduced, and more and more housing—the new housing built by the Revolution—was made

[23]Bernardo, *Theory of Moral Incentives*, pp. 54–55.
[24]Fidel Castro, speech of December 9, 1967, in *Granma* (December 12, 1967): 3.
[25]Castro, speech of July 26, 1968, in *Granma* (July 28, 1968): 4.
[26]Fidel Castro, May 1, 1971, quoted in David Barkin, "The Redistribution of Consumption in Cuba," in Barkin and Manitzas (eds.) *Cuba*, pp. 95–96.

available, distributed without charge through an allocational system tied primarily to the need for workers in various places. Food prices were controlled, and almost all food, in any case, sharply rationed. Medical care was distributed free and also made much more generally accessible by a push to develop clinics and hospitals in the rural areas which, before the Revolution, represented both the very low end of the income distribution and the areas lacking in social services. The same was true even more strikingly of education; by 1970, over a quarter of the population was in schools,[27] not only tuition-free, but in large part boarding institutions providing also board and room (with the student's ration card remaining with the family as an implicit stimulus to enrollment). Funerals were paid for by the state. Those who wished to have a traditional wedding were free to do so, but the incentives for a less religious and more socialist formula were powerful: the chance to have one's wedding solemnized, without charge, in the ornate mansion rechristened the Palace of Matrimony, with use of one of the salons for the reception and an aging but polished Cadillac, also provided by the state, to sweep the newly wedded couple away after the ceremony. (We spent a happy three-quarters of an hour watching outside as the couples came off the nuptial assembly line.)

(I also watched later, in the airport of Mexico City, the face of the woman coming from Havana who was realizing that she was now in a country where one had to put money into the telephone for a local call.)

At the same time, the resources that monetary income could command were becoming so scarce that money was losing its value. Power over people was delivered through

[27]Barkin and Manitzas, 1973, p. 87.

the political-administrative system. Money could still buy goods—but there were almost no goods to be bought. Dry-goods stores displayed empty shelves. Cosmetics were scarce and available only on ration. Refreshment bars rarely had coffee or soft drinks. With the black market, observers seem to agree, reasonably well-controlled, money income could hardly buy anything more consequential than a dinner at a good restaurant, or a dish of ice cream at the ornate Coppelia ice-cream parlor. Money could also, for a time at least, buy one option to waiting in line for even these limited pleasures, for the inflationary pressure produced by full employment in a drastic scarcity of consumer goods produced long lines for even such modest pleasures as ice cream and restaurant meals, and with these, for a time, persons who specialized in selling places in lines.[28] Every night, while we were in Havana in 1968, we watched people standing, an average of two and a half hours in the ice-cream lines—a way of spending an evening out, and rather a social event. People joked: "If they put the national debt on sale, a line would form."

It is argued that "when consumer goods are scarce, small differences assume great importance and create attitudes that reinforce the desire for material goods."[29] The long lines at the ice-cream parlor seem to substantiate this. And yet, it seemed at that time that the economy of nonmaterial incentives was able to grow in large part simply because of the absence of competing rewards for action. Coming from the United States, where the unprecedented number and volume of material goods seemed hardly to have blunted interest in them, the reign of moral incentives appeared a good deal

[28]C. Mesa-Lago, "Cuba" p. 97.
[29]Silverman, *Man and Socialism*, p. 24.

more plausible in the Cuban economy of scarcity than in Marx's projected future abundance.

Certainly the revolutionary leadership was not relying simply on the disappearance of one set of prizes and the generation of an alternative set. Cubans moved in a world created or restructured so as to develop a new kind of psychic economy. Society was envisioned as, almost in its totality, a vast educational enterprise for the creation of the New Man.

Besides the voluntary organizations like the Federation of Women, and, most important of course, the Party itself, there were the little neighborhood Committees for the Defense of the Revolution that collected trash, planted coffee in vacant lots, looked out for those who needed social services— and, very clearly, served to control, discipline, pressure those whose actions showed them as lacking in revolutionary consciousness. The many boarding schools with the students housed in dormitories, eating collectively, receiving their clothing and books from the revolutionary government, and discussing together each other's faults and achievements as group members (or so, at least, students do at the Makarenko teacher-training institution, I was told there), are institutions for shaping a new kind of social character. So too were the day-care institutions, with their stress on collective activity. We witnessed a trial in one of the new "popular tribunals" where small delicts are tried by a panel of locally elected judges; the judges are neighbors; evidence is not limited to the specific transgressions but may touch on general aspects of the accused's character; there is no protection against self-incrimination—in short, the intent of the process is social control through internalization of a standard of conduct, not through "justice" in the English or American sense.

The institutions of work are treated as instruments for building consciousness. Factories are organized in a structure of committees involving a mix of workers, party members, and technical leadership at each level; goals (which, of course, come down from the top) are discussed, all the way down and up again, both as a way of getting needed information flow and more effective planning of the work, and as a way of developing commitment. Worker participation in electing some of their fellows to the advance-guard movements is another form of political participation.

The major reeducative practice in the Cuban system was that of voluntary work, in a variety of forms. It could take place in the context of a neighborhood, with the Committee for the Defense of the Revolution organizing the planting of coffee on some vacant lot; of an organization, as when the Federation of Women led a group of women out to plant in the agricultural *cordon* around Havana; of a school, with children out in the country to work in agriculture for a period; of a government office, as when a group of bureaucrats from the Ministry of Justice went out from the city to spend several weeks or months on the farm for which that agency had the responsibility. On the Isle of Pines, thousands of young Cubans, receiving a nominal wage and living in barracks with their food, clothing, transport, books "according to need," built dams, planted trees, erected schools, and formed a small model of the society to come.

Voluntary work was often highly dramatized, taking on the character of a communal rite or festival. It is probably in these work gatherings that the Cuban enterprise displayed itself most strongly as "a revolution with the atmosphere of a socialist carnival."[30] Volunteer work had its annual focus—both crisis and culmination—in the yearly sugarcane harvest

[30]Dumont, *Cuba*, p. 87.

in which the still unmechanized cutting of the cane meant that human beings, farmers, bureaucrats, students, women, would have to go through fields as large as an American wheatfield cutting the tough cane stalk by stalk by machete—with afterward the meetings, the songs, and the medals.

Voluntary overtime has obvious economic functions. What sort of wage bill would it have taken to mobilize a large segment of the relatively highly paid urban work force for the most back-breaking and man-demeaning job in the Cuban economy? Unpaid overtime makes every kind of sense in an economy of consumer-goods shortages and rising inflationary pressure.[31]

For Guevara, it is clear, the choice of moral incentives was very deeply rooted in a basic conception of the nature of the Revolution:

> We are fighting against misery, but we are also fighting against alienation. One of the fundamental objectives of Marxism is to remove interest, the factor of individual interest, and gain from men's psychological motivations. Marx was preoccupied both with economic factors and with their repercussions on the spirit. If communism isn't interested in this, too, it may be a method of distributing goods, but it will never be a revolutionary way of life.[32]

But Guevara did not win the Great Debate; no one did. It was not until later that Castro placed himself, and with the statement the course of the Revolution, squarely on the side of

---

[31]It has been calculated that during the years 1962-1967 the salaries "saved" by unpaid labor amounted to an average of $50 million each year, or about 1.4% of the annual national income: Carmelo Mesa-Lago, "Tipología y valor económico del trabajo no renumerado en Cuba," *El Trimestre Economico* 40, no. 3 (July–September, 1973): 707.

[32]Quoted in Silverman, *Man and Socialism*, p. 5.

using awareness to create wealth. Perhaps circumstances won the debate.

For the Cuban Revolution was set a task which it is hard to imagine could have been solved by the material incentives available. It had to accumulate capital, first to develop agriculture, and later, after increasing agricultural productivity, to transfer the agricultural surplus into capitalizing industry. The only possible source of capital appeared to be sugar, a crop which it was not yet possible to mechanize. The transformation of the economy had replaced the unemployment of the years before the Revolution by labor shortages. How could labor be mobilized for agriculture without that army of unemployed who had waited out the "dead season" before the Revolution?[33] Saving for the future meant that Cubans would have to do without goods in the present. How could people be mobilized to work when work could not entitle them to the consumer goods which were not to be had? As Castro put it, "Are we going to stimulate the people with money with which they can buy nothing?"[34] The Revolution made of work a social duty, a personal commitment, part of a "socialist carnival."

It is not possible to use the Cuban experience definitively to confirm or disprove Che Guevara's contention that the development of consciousness does more for development of production in a relatively short time than material incentives do, because adequate statistics on the overall performance of the Cuban economy are conspicuously lacking and because there were plenty of reasons other than the system of incen-

[33]See B. H. Pollitt, "Employment Plans, Performance, and Future Prospects in Cuba," in *Third World Employment: Problems and Strategies*, eds. Richard Jolly et al. (Harmondsworth: Penguin Books, 1973).
[34]Quoted in Mesa-Lago, 1971, "Cuba," p. 83.

tives for the Cuban economy to have had its difficulties.[35] The general sense of easing up in the seventies appears to be not only the result of the high price of sugar but a payoff of the high level of investment, including investment in human resources, which went before.[36] But moral incentives have brought their problems.

Voluntary work is often inefficient. The often-caustic René Dumont tells us:

> The 41,300 volunteer coffee harvesters from the province of Oriente, many of them scholarship students, gathered only 7.8 per cent of the total harvest in 1962, Mestre emphasizes. And they picked an average of 1.06 boxes of coffee berries per day, as against an average of seven boxes for a large group of good workers. Since they managed to pick only one-twelfth of what a good harvester picks, and one seventh of what a very average worker picks, they did not even pay back the amount spent for their food, lodging and transportation. Moreover, such a slow pace provokes various reactions and uncomplimentary remarks, on the part of workers used to such jobs.[37]

Even if performed efficiently, volunteer work, thought of as "free" or costless, is not always used efficiently in the productive system. Bertram Silverman summarizes some observations on this point:

> Thus moral incentives have served to compensate for the inefficiencies and irrationalities of the economic organization. Indeed, moral incentives often foster the irrational uses of labor and capital, since managers do not

[35]Bernardo, *Theory of Moral Incentives*, pp. 99–118; Mesa-Lago, "Tipología y valor," pp. 105–109.
[36]Barkin, "Popular Participation."
[37]Dumont, *Cuba*, p. 88.

feel compelled to complete tasks that could be done during the normal work day. Nor do they feel compelled to explore sources of inefficiency. Administrators frequently considered overtime or voluntary work costless, and were often perplexed when asked whether they had wasted *conciencia* in fulfilling their goals. The same attitude was prevalent in agriculture. Since no production unit assumed the cost of voluntary work, more labor was frequently demanded than was needed in order to guarantee results. Often the irrational use of moral incentives results in problems of worker apathy and discontent. The cost of *conciencia* (Cuba's most precious resource) needs to be considered.[38]

Moreover, it could be argued that Cuban workers, deprived of the material incentives of pay raises or overtime pay, or having these rendered meaningless by lack of material goods, have been issuing themselves leisure—which one might call one sort of material incentive. Pointing to a Cuban report in 1969 that wage claims had been substantially reduced while claims resulting from absenteeism, negligence, and lack of discipline had increased sharply, Mesa-Lago hypothesizes: "The scarcity of consumer goods could be the main reason behind the decline in wage claims in a society in which money is becoming less and less important," and finds corroboration in a report on absenteeism released by the Party Commission on Revolutionary Orientation that attributed absenteeism largely to the circumstance that "there is more money in circulation than things on which to spend it. Every worker knows that he can live on what he is paid for working 15 or 20 days a month."[39]

Castro's remarkable speech after the failure of the 1970

---

[38]Silverman, *"Economic Organization: Some Dilemmas,"* pp. 413–14.
[39]Mesa-Lago 972, *op.cit.,* pp. 91–92.

cane harvest to meet the goal of ten million tons—already in 1968 the theme of a vast campaign of exhortation—displays the difficulties that can arise when labor is allocated in a system of moral incentives.[40] The lack of coordination and the misallocation of resources had been such, Castro concluded, that the heroic effort in the sugar harvest had actually increased the economic difficulties of the Cuban economy.

The failure of the ten-million-ton harvest led the leadership of the Revolution to a thoroughgoing reevaluation of the moral-incentive system. The result was policy changes at many levels: the tying of wages more closely to productivity: legal penalties against loafing and absenteeism: the provision of a greater amount and variety of consumer goods; the reorganization of the governmental structure toward greater decentralization and participation. The politicizing of work was still to be a central theme, and some of the allocation of material incentives like houses and bicycles is, under the new policies, handled through collective, participatory institutions. But in some important sense the "moral-incentives" strategy of the late sixties has been judged inefficient.[41]

Yet what sense does it make to evaluate the Cuban economy in traditional economic terms? The Revolution joined nationalism, economic development, and social justice; its political economy was based on a view that saw these objectives as aspects of a single process. It created social institutions built around work, and economic institutions built around the transformation of society and social conscience. Billboards I saw in 1968 urged Cubans on to "Ten Million Tons in 1970";

[40]Fidel Castro, speech of July 26, 1970, in *Granma* (August 2, 1970): 2–6; and comments of Carmelo Mesa-Lago, "Tipología y valor económico," pp. 707–708.
[41]Karl, "Work Incentives."

they also urged "More Revolution." Revolution was to be also a product of the Cuban economic system. As Bernardo says, at the very end of his somewhat pessimistic evaluation of moral incentives:

> Moral stimulation was not implemented solely as a mobilizer of effort and skills for a massive investment effort but as a social invention to replace the old socio-moral norms inherited from the past. That egalitarianism was valued greatly by the leaders is shown in their early hasty efforts at eliminating overt unemployment quickly; by their policy of reallocating resources in favor of the countryside; by the extension of opportunities to racial minorities, women and children. Egalitarianism may be considered a non-material output of the Cuban productive system alongside more familiar material outputs such as butter and barbering.[42]

In producing equality, the Cuban system has done very well.

One of the uses of voluntary labor was to break down the class barriers which in pre-Revolutionary Cuba had separated city dweller from *campesino*, and the members of the privileged middle class from those who worked with their hands. Bureaucrats from the Ministry of Justice are probably not very efficient farmers; it was in the interests of social equality that they planted coffee and cut cane with the rest.

Moreover, to have people donating their labor is a way of developing commitment to the Revolution, and to have them donating their labor in groups was a way of developing a stronger collective sense. The work parties in the cane field or on the coffee plantation were as much social ritual, a kind of communion, as they were activities with material ends. Indeed, the politicized economy of Cuba had in 1968 as much the flavor of a religious movement as of an economic system.

[42]Bernardo, *Theory of Moral Incentives*, p. 152.

The Revolution has its shrines—the Moncada Barracks, with its photographic exhibit and its bullet-pocked walls, the Siboney farmhouse where the attack started, with its pictures and its carefully preserved uniforms and shoes of the attackers; Raúl Castro's command post of the Second Front; the little museum at Playa Giron with more photographs of the invasion and the carefully preserved American war material. It has its martyrs; they are called by that term, and reminders of them are everywhere. Every factory, every school, every state farm, every sugar mill, is named for some *martir* of the Revolution. Looking at the names and the posters and at photograph after photograph of bodies beaten, bodies bloodied, bodies castrated or eyes gouged out, I thought of what the Catholic Church has always said: "The blood of the martyrs is the seed of the Church." And this Revolution, so like a religious movement, has also its collective rituals: not only the great assemblages with Castro speaking, but those volunteer work parties which were, like the rituals of a church, both the sign of and the means to what Catholic theology would call a "state of grace."[43]

It was this atmosphere of Movement that made Cuba in 1968 so exhilarating to an American. Yet this system has its costs, which are not merely the inefficiencies previously mentioned. It is not possible to support strongly and develop certain motives without weakening and blunting others. The cost paid for collective consciousness is also in some kinds of individual expression.

A system organized to make men feel in their work a powerful joy in participation in the collective enterprise of society is not conducive to work involving a great deal of

[43]Lisa R. Peattie, "Cuban Notes," *Massachusetts Review* (November 1969), pp. 652–674.

introspection, or the expression of a powerful, idiosyncratic creative drive. I am in no position to evaluate the literary or artistic output of the Revolution, and certainly we saw, besides a brilliant poster art, a Cuban-made motion picture, *Memorias del Subdesarrollo*, both powerful and almost troublingly introspective in its character. But we had some interesting discussions about the building of the School of Art with a young architect, who compared their dramatic brilliance unfavorably with a small pavilion of his own. "It is not that Porro's buildings are romantic; it is that they are so personal— he has built a monument to himself. They have supporters and opponents. My pavilion has no opponents. It has people who like it, and people who do not notice it but who are satisfied there."[44]

A society that collectivizes on the Cuban model is simply not going to support—perhaps not even permit—certain kinds of very individualistic work.

A system of moral incentives is compatible with a great deal of economic decentralization—as the Chinese experiment demonstrates—and it is certainly compatible with a great deal of individual initiative and individual resourcefulness in problem solving. (Again, the Chinese system, with its size, its decentralization, and its strategy of "walking on two legs"— developing small, labor-intensive enterprises along with the larger more capital-intensive ones—is particularly rich in examples; for a vivid account, see the report of Wheelwright and McFarlane.[45]) But this kind of creative energy was evident in the Cuban system too, even though, according to one writer

it is symptomatic that the type of production that is dis-

[44]*Ibid.*, pp. 672–673.
[45]E. I. Wheelwright and Bruce McFarlane, *The Chinese Road to Socialism: Economics of the Cultural Revolution* (New York: Monthly Review Press, 1971).

persed and requires a large number of manual workers whose output is difficult to control (e.g., sugar, coffee and tobacco plantations, cattle-raising and the like) is the one showing the poorest performance. On the other hand, certain operations that can be easily concentrated and operated with a small number of skilled, well-disciplined workers (e.g., fish and egg production) are the ones showing increase in output.[46]

Nor can a moral incentives system like the Cuban one be said to "stifle discussion"; work and events are continually being discussed, and the general level of articulateness is, again, one of the exhilarating features of such a system. But such a system certainly does not encourage dissent, or alternative views of the nature of things. To structure society as a single vast educational enterprise for the creation of the New Man is to link all the institutions together in a common stream of thought. The institutional bases for competing views have been systematically taken away in the interests of consensus and social commitment; schools, voluntary organizations, and trade unions have been linked together by the revolutionary leadership so that all social energies may flow in the same channel. The student representatives who in the university structure sit on every level of university administration up to the very top participate in its management, but not as representatives of the special interests of students; they participate in the enterprise of getting student commitment to the goals of the Revolution through their work in the university.

By 1968, the Cuban labor movement had practically ceased to exist,[47] and workers' organizations in the factory

---

[46]Mesa-Lago, 1972, "Cuba" p. 95.

[47]See K. S. Karol, *Guerrillas in Power: The Course of the Cuban Revolution* (New York: Hill & Wang, 1970), for a painstaking critique of this process as it applies to organized labor.

did not function to articulate the special interests of workers but to organize workers to fulfill, more effectively, societal goals. Under the new political strategies that followed 1970, the unions are being revived, but in a framework which ensures that they will be a strand in the movement of the Revolution, not a special-interest advocate.[48]

An American visitor, exhilarated, as I have said, by the commitment and social energy in the Cuban system, could still be frightened at the centralism inherent in the political system that structures and is supported by that commitment. At least one Marxist critic of the system has gone so far as to see the whole Cuban ideology of "moral incentives" as a rationalization of a sort of group interest of the revolutionary leadership:

> This is the effect of an ideology and a political line which concentrates all power in the hands of a ruling group, and which therefore, do not create the necessary conditions—ideological, organizational and political—for the democratic exercise of proletarian power . . . it is related to political domination by a "radicalized" section of the petty bourgeoisie.[49]

The Cuban system in 1968 felt to me frighteningly centralized; it did not feel repressive. Relatively few people to whom we spoke seemed to harbor substantial resentments against the leadership—and those who did appeared astonishingly free to tell us what they thought; the Cubans did not act like frightened people, and a leadership that permits guns to be widely distributed among the general population cannot

[48]Marifeli Perez-Stable, "Whither the Cuban Working-Class," *Latin American Perspectives,* issue 7, supplement 1975, vol. II, no. 4.
[49]Charles Bettelheim, "On the Transition Between Capitalism and Socialism," *Monthly Review,* 20 (March 1969): 1–10.

be afraid of its people. What kept the system, with all its centralism, from being repressive? One was the style of leadership connected with what in China is called the "mass line"—accessible, antitechnocratic (with the costs which this entails for "rational planning"), and minimizing differences of status between leader and led. Castro and the rest of the bureaucrats sweat in the sun as they cut cane; Castro in rumpled fatigues may appear anywhere in his jeep to argue with a group of bus drivers or to take a personal interest in the problems of a poor farming family outside Havana and order them a new house *immediately*; or, in 1970, when the cane harvest failed to meet its targets, present the problems of the Cuban economy to the people of Cuba in that extraordinarily frank speech. The system is nourished by information flow up and down.

But behind the very possibility of this extraordinary leadership style lies a basic fact: the positive aspects of the "moral incentives" system can dominate so long as faith in the movement is general—but the positive incentives can dominate only as long as they do in fact serve to motivate the members of society. The Revolution is tied to economic development, and its leaders cannot afford to fail in the task of mobilizing and organizing work. Back of every system of positive incentives is a negative set; the hunger and sense of personal failure that are, at different levels, the penalties of the market system have their counterparts in the administrated penalties of the authoritarian "command economy." If conscience fails, then compulsion is likely to take its place, and the system of institutions developed to produce conscience will have, if they are turned to compulsion, very great potential for repression.

Hans Koningsberger, recording a visit to China, muses: "Perhaps we should not talk about capitalism versus communism, but about a 'money society' versus a 'rules soci-

ety.' " "A rules society"—in this phrase he places the Cuban
and Chinese system with those simpler preindustrial economies around which anthropologists have built their thought.
Then he goes on to say: "Such a rules society could function
best in isolation."[50]

This poses another of the problems for the Cuban system.
It is not simply a problem of the "ideological erosion" which
comes from contact with other systems—the sort of contact
and example that has built pressure for consumer goods
among the socialist countries of Eastern Europe. There is the
market itself as it enters through the international division of
labor:

> For a small, foreign-oriented country an unmistakable
> yardstick of efficiency makes its presence known im-
> mediately in the form of declining foreign exchange earn-
> ings caused by a resulting reduction in the volume of
> exports and falling terms of trade. . . . The notion of
> foregone foreign exchange introduces cost consciousness
> in the planners, facilitating the ranking and evaluation
> of investment alternatives in a more businesslike, effi-
> cient, and quantifiable manner. Finally, such a country
> requires flexibility at the periphery in adapting to chang-
> ing technologies and tastes in foreign markets.[51]

The Cuban experiment can fail in more than one way.
It can fail from its own inherent problems and contradictions;
it can fail from the irremovable circumstances to which it must
adapt. "Men make their own history, but they do not make
it just as they please."[52] But for some years, at least, the

[50]Hans Koningsberger, *Love and Hate in China* (London: Jonathan Cape, 1966),
p. 118.
[51]Bernardo, *Theory of Moral Incentives*, p. 129.
[52]Robert C. Tucker (ed.), *The Marx–Engels Reader* (New York: W. W. Norton,
1978), p. 595.

Revolution has been an instance of men acting as though they could make their history, and treating the necessity of working to live as a field of social and moral activity.

The Cuban and Chinese systems, for better or for worse, are attempts at doing, in industrialized economies, what Karl Polanyi asked for when he said: "I plead for the restoration of that unity of motives which should inform man in his every day activity as a producer, for the reabsorption of the economic system in society, for the creative adaption of our ways of life to an industrial environment."[53]

I do not know what Karl Polanyi would have thought of Cuba.

The "unity of motives" which we find in the small, isolated, slowly-changing folk society we call "cultural integration," and we think of it as the product of circumstances and history, not of human will. When it appears as the product of a society like Cuba, we understand that it is the product of intent and of deliberate human action. We may evaluate that intent and action as the work of creating a new and nobler society. Or we may emphasize the downplaying of individual expression that goes along with building a "unity of motives." But I think it is generally sensed that the pressures of the development process will lead human societies more in the direction of "societal planning" than away from it, and that therefore the Cuban Revolution, an extraordinary social experiment in a very small country, has some general importance for us all.

The Cuban case is at one end of a continuum: the building of an extraordinary society. Yet it brings out themes that are

---

[53]Karl Polanyi, "Our Obsolete Market Mentality," in *Primitive, Archaic and Modern Economies*, ed. George Dalton (Boston: Beacon Press, 1968), pp. 72–73.

likely to be recurrent. The Revolution moralized work partly
for reasons of ideology, growing out of concern with equality
and the reduction of alienation; the Revolution also moralized
work in the service of technical efficiency, so as to mobilize
productive forces under central planning. All these are likely
to be issues that recur in societies which may start from quite
different premises. The pressure for greater equality, which
has been one of the major political phenomena of our time,
is not likely to go away; a concern for the *quality* of life, including work life, it is here argued is likely, for several reasons, to increase. The need for mobilization and for a political
ideology that can justify an increased importance for planning
are also likely to be recurrent phenomena. Thus the forces
that made work, for the Cuban Revolution, part of the moral
as well as the technical order are likely to operate elsewhere
as well.

Chapter 6 / FAMILY
IN DEVELOPMENT

In the last section we considered how the moral order and the technical order have been joined by bringing a part of the technical order—work—into the sphere of the political life, and making it a central part of the system of social meaning. But the reverse may also take place; the "personal," the "cultural," the "moral" affect the technical order, and may be deliberately shaped with that relevance in view. Here we shall attempt to show how a social element generally thought to be quite outside the technical order—the family—can play a part in that order.

There is a great deal of literature that deals with the consequences of economic development—or of certain of its aspects, such as industrialization and urbanization—for the family and more generally the institutions of kinship. Less common is any attempt to say what the nature of the family *should* be, as part of some overall development strategy. Yet there have been some attempts in this direction too, at least implicitly, and the forms and functions of the family are surely relevant to the processes of development.

The family has a critical role in the rate of population growth, one variable at least that is taken explicitly into account in economic planning.

It is a critical institution of socialization of the young for the future; there are choices to be made as to the degree to which the shaping of the new generation will be left to families, or turned over to competing institutions.

The family may be an important unit of resource management; in peasant agriculture, it is typically *the* primary productive unit. Even where production is organized through other institutions, it is likely still to be a basic unit of consumption.

In many societies, the family still serves as the primary welfare system, the cushion for uncertainty in the labor market.

Finally, the family may have a sort of negative or balancing role in the system—as a center for interest which can compete with, balance, or, alternatively, blend in with other institutions, political and economic.

To what extent is the family likely to endure? And in what form? And for what functions? To what extent should the organization of life through kinship be encouraged, or be rendered obsolete? What should policy be toward the family as part of a strategy of economic development?

The more one thinks about this theme, the more interesting appear the questions, and the less easy their answers; in the first place, because the relationships between the various sorts of kinship arrangements and the possibilities of economic activity are not well understood, and, in the second place, because it is clear that there is not one single road to "modernity," and that various societies will have their own forms of development and their own futures. Nevertheless, it may be useful to open up a discussion of the theme as one way of thinking about the interrelationships of institutions in building the future.

Primitive societies tend to be organized in very large part through the institutions of kinship. When technology changes slowly, when mobility is minimal, when the span of organization is small, when the major elements in the division of labor are the natural categories of age and sex, kinship relations can easily play a major role in all the activities of life, including economic ones.

In peasant agriculture, the family is the basic unit of production, as well as of consumption. In preindustrial societies, other productive activities are often carried out in the same family-enterprise pattern, with outsiders, if they are involved in the enterprise, assimilated into a structure of relationships dominated by and modeled on those of the family.

Peter Laslett begins his account of "the world we have lost" with an account of a London bakery of the year 1619:

> There were thirteen or fourteen people in such an undertaking: the baker and his wife, four paid employees who were called journeymen, two apprentices, two maidservants and three or four children of the master baker himself. Six pounds ten shillings a week was reckoned to be the outgoing of this establishment, of which only eleven shillings and eightpence went for wages; half a crown a week for each of the journeymen and tenpence for each of the maids. Far and away the greatest expense was for food. . . . Clothing was charged up too,

not only for the man, wife and children, but for the apprentices as well. Even school fees were claimed as a justifiable charge on the price of bread for sale.

A London bakery was undoubtedly what we should call a commercial or even an industrial undertaking turning out loaves by the thousand. Yet the business was carried on in the house of the baker himself. . . .

The only word used at that time to describe such a group of people was "family." The man at the head of the group, the entrepreneur, the employer, or the manager, was then known as the master or head of the family. He was father to some of its members and in place of father to the rest. There was no sharp distinction between his domestic and his economic functions. His wife was both his partner and his subordinate, a partner because she ran the family, took charge of the food and managed the women-servants, a subordinate because she was woman and wife, mother and in place of mother to the rest.[1]

The first stages of the industrial revolution in England did not at once destroy the pattern of work within household units. The spinning mills were tied to an expanding weaving industry taking place in households, and the development of the first mass market for furniture and clothing created not furniture and clothing factories but the dreadful sweated trades of parents and children working at home which Mayhew describes so movingly.[2] For a time, and to a degree, the kinship organization of labor even moved into the new factories:

[1]Peter Laslett, *The World We Have Lost* (London: Methuen & Co., 1971), pp. 1–2.
[2]*The Unknown Mayhew*, ed. E. P. Thompson and Eileen Yeo (Harmondsworth: Penguin Books, 1973).

Witnesses before the parliamentary committees from 1816 through 1819 testified consistently that masters allowed the operative spinners to hire their own assistants (piecers, scavengers, etc.) and that the spinners chose their wives, children, near relatives, or relatives of the proprietors. Many children, especially the youngest, entered the mill at the express request of their parents. . . .

In general the spinner paid his assistants from his own wages; the master did not deal with the assistants at all. Adult spinners preferred this system both because they could supplement their own family wages by their children's labor and because, as one spinner put it, "working in a cottonmill I could instruct them myself in their work."[3]

Nevertheless, the new industrial organization could not but disarrange seriously the structure of the family:

The recruitment of women and children weakened the traditional domestic basis for child-rearing. Because the opportunities for the adult male in the industry were limited, his status as chief breadwinner in the family was in danger. Furthermore, it was becoming harder for him to train his children for a trade.[4]

It was not until the system—with a substantial push from the organization of labor—had evolved to a pattern of shorter hours, higher wages, and curtailment of child labor that the working-class family could settle into a new pattern with the male as breadwinner and other members sharing in the consumption of his earnings.

There is general agreement that in the life of the "developed" societies the family and kinship play a much less

[3]Neil J. Smelser, *Social Change in the Industrial Revolution: An Application of Theory to the Lancashire Cotton Industry 1770-1840* (London: Routledge & Kegan Paul, 1959), pp. 189–90.
[4]*Ibid.*, p. 188.

important role within the whole; this difference was at the center of Maine's contrast between societies of "status" and those of "contract," or of Tonnies's *Gemeinschaft* and *Gesellschaft*. Other institutions appear which do not exist in simpler societies. There are specialized religious, political, educational, and economic institutions that serve some of the functions organized in the simpler societies exclusively by the family group and other institutions of kinship. The state regulates the relations between family members. Economic enterprises, on the other hand, hire, fire, and promote not families, but individuals.

From time to time, it is prophesied that the family as an institution is on the way to disappearance. An American mass-circulation magazine announced in 1948 that

> the U.S. family, deep in the millrace of social and technological change, is itself deep in trouble. . . .
> Today the forces of social change have. . . . broken down the family. It is now tiny—a husband, a wife and one or two children. Its members do little more than eat and sleep together. They buy everything—food, laundry, entertainment—and produce nothing but the money for these purchases. The outward pull of movies, automobiles, bridge clubs, and Elks constantly threaten what little family unity remains. The individual now looks outside his home for his interests. He is atomistic, an individualized fragment rather than a part of a unified whole.[5]

But there is a great deal of evidence to the effect that, if the family is going to disappear, it has not yet done so. To the large sociological literature that tended to treat the family

[5]*Life*, July 26, 1948, pp. 83–99. *Selected Studies in Marriage and the Family*, ed. Robert F. Winch and Robert McGinnis (New York: Henry Holt & Co., 1953) pp. 18–19.

as an institution in decline, there has been added in recent years a number of studies that show kinship relations as very much alive in a number of urban settings. The Boston Italians described by Herbert Gans in *The Urban Villagers*[6] might be thought of as peasants transplanted, people leading in the West End of Boston a kind of family-focused life developed in another time and place, and not yet modified for a changed setting. But the people of the London slums studied by Michael Young and Peter Willmott,[7] with their continual interchange of contact and small attentions between Mum and her daughters, had been city people for generations. Even members of the mobile middle class turn out to maintain a good deal of interaction with relatives outside the nuclear household.[8]

Even in economic activity, the family still plays some role. If we take the United States as a type of "developed" economy, we see that the economic heights are held by great corporate bureaucracies, that a major part of food is produced not by small family farms but by "factories in the field," and that the chain supermarkets make survival difficult for the Mom and Pop grocery. Even so, "family ownership in the organization itself . . . is quite typical of most American farming, much of retail and service employment and the top echelons in middle-sized business."[9] A fairly recent study of the

[6]Herbert Gans, *The Urban Villagers: Group and Class in the Life of Italian-Americans* (New York: Free Press, 1962).

[7]Michael Young and Peter Willmott, *Family and Kinship in East London* (London: Routledge & Kegan Paul, 1957).

[8]E. Litwak, "Occupational Mobility and Extended Family Cohesion," and "Geographical Mobility and Extended Family Cohesion," *American Sociological Review*, 26 (1960): 9, 385.

[9]A. L. Stinchcombe, "Social Structure and the Intervention of Organizational Forms," in *Industrial Man*, ed. Tom Burns (Harmondsworth: Penguin Books, 1969), p. 187.

116 | CHAPTER 6

British boot and shoe industry revealed it as largely one of family-controlled enterprises.[10] Even within the corporate heights there are the Fords and Du Ponts.

Most interesting of all is the argument in a recent study that in the United States, just as production moved out of the household into the market economy in the early part of the Industrial Revolution, some kinds are now moving back into the household. The small family unit that was not competitive with the factory in much goods production is quite competitive in services; meanwhile, the rise in labor costs and the income-tax structure provide strong incentives for the family members to do for themselves what another generation would have paid to have done for them.[11]

So "modernity" does not seem to mean that kinship and the family cease to have any importance. But this is not the same as arguing that kinship structures have an important role in the social and economic transformation that we call development. It may be that kinship ties, no longer part of the economic system that has been taken over, as it were, by new institutions, continue to persist for a time, because the process is not yet complete, or because they serve certain irreducible and nontransferable social or psychological functions, a necessary cost of running an otherwise economically rational system. Or there is an alternative view: that the processes in the "technical order," which we call "development," make use of, and require, informal and quite unofficial institutions, including some sorts of families.

The view that is taken of the role of kinship in the de-

[10]H. A. Silverman (ed.), "The Boot and Shoe Industry" in *Studies in Industrial Organization* (London: Methuen and Co., 1946).
[11]Scott Burns *Home, Inc., The Hidden Wealth and Power of the American Household* (Garden City, N.Y.: Doubleday & Co., 1975).

velopment process will depend in part on the view taken as to the relative roles of the state and the private spheres. A society like that of Cuba that has taken as the central theme of its development process a massive social mobilization and a general resocialization to new values is bound to downplay the family, with its placing of the young under the conservative influence of the parental generation. The family as an institution of socialization and object of allegiance competes with allegiance to broader social units. The collective child-rearing institutions of the Israeli kibbutzim were in part a way of freeing women for productive work and collective defense, and of rationalizing and reducing consumption in the interests of collective investment, but it was also a way of reducing the development of loyalties competing with those to the kibbutz and the maximizing of informal control over kibbutz members. The children's houses were economically efficient, but there was more to it than that: "The children belonged to the community as a whole.[12]

Furthermore, the family as an institution that controls resources is one that promotes inequality. A society that permits families to hold important sources of wealth, and to pass them on to their heirs, is promoting inequality between families and between the individuals who are members of differentially endowed families. Socialist suspicion of the family also reflects a strong commitment to equality.

The view taken will depend as well on what one sees as the critical barriers to development.

Talcott Parsons and his followers who see the essence of modern socioeconomic systems in the rational allocation of human resources—status achieved through individual effort,

[12]Yonina Talmon, *Family and Community in the Kibbutz* (Cambridge: Harvard University Press, 1972), p. 8.

rather than ascribed on the basis of race, caste, and family background, relationships functionally specific, and the criteria for social placement universalistic ones like skill rather than personal characteristics—naturally see any broad extension of kinship as standing in the way of progress. In this view, the logic of modern economic organization leads directly to the conjugal, or nuclear, family with but one member (the family head) seriously involved in the economic system; the personalistic relations within the family serving the economy indirectly, by socializing the young for future struggle in the competitive economy.

In this perspective, the family (again, the conjugal family) is outside the technical economic order, and functions as a contrast to it, a personal world that can heal the wounds of economic competition. In the words of William Goode:

> At any level, the enterprise has no responsibility for the emotional input—output of the family, in the sense that there is nowhere else to go for it. The small family, then, deals with a problem which the industrial system cannot handle . . . without a family unit to deal with the idiosyncrasies of aged parents, the emotional needs of adults, or the insecurities of children, very likely not enough adequately functioning people would be produced to man the industrial system.[13]

But suppose one does not see the essence of modern institutions as bureaucratic rationality? Suppose one sees the requirements of the development process as resources, plus motivations, plus institutions—and takes the position that social institutions are often cemented together by very non-rational elements. Then one would take a very different view

[13]William J. Goode, *The Family* (Englewood Cliffs, N.J.: Prentice-Hall, 1964) p. 109.

as to the place of kinship institutions in the development process.

As one critic of Parsonian ideas in this area puts it

> The basic requirements of industrialization, it would be generally agreed, are a surplus of capital, the requisite financial instutitions, willingness to employ capital in productive uses on the basis of maximizing its return, enough people and/or good enough communications to constitute a mass market and provide a labour force, an educated *elite* capable of technological innovation, a set of ideas which will legitimize the activities of control and coordination of productive processes, and a surplus of agricultural produce.[14]

Successful industrialization, he goes on to say, does not require that people begin to act in the rational, "universalistic" way proposed by Parsons's conception of the modern economy. If such ideas do seem to be associated with industrialization, it may well be because of their ideological function "in the initial stages of serving to legitimize the authority of the industrialising elite."[15]

In fact, it appears quite unlikely that economic institutions of this rational "bureaucratic" character would appear to any substantial degree in the early stages of the development process. The presenting issues in at least the early stages of the development process may not be so much the institutionalization of universalistic and achievement values, as the development of going institutions on some basis—perhaps that of the family.

Indeed, everyone's favorite success story in the economic

[14]C. C. Harris, *The Family: An Introduction* (London: George Allen & Unwin, 1969), p. 113.
[15]*Ibid.*, p. 113.

development field—Japan—appears to have done it largely by basing its economic institutions on existing family groupings. James Abbegglen has pointed out that the very successful industries of Japan have been organized according to a set of principles very different from the universalistic, individualistic line that—at the level of ideology at least—characterize those of the United States.

> The Japanese factory is like such other Japanese social groups as the family in terms of the commitment of members of the group, the nature of recruitment to the group and subsequent careers, and the extent of involvement of members with each other as part of the group. Although a factory might be, and in the West tends to be, defined narrowly as an economic organization, with relationships based on contribution to productivity and profit, the Japanese factory is not so defined. In Japan the factory recruits, involves and maintains its membership on a basis similar to that of the domestic and social groups in the society. Where the economic goals of the factory conflict with this broader definition of the group's goals, the economic ends take a secondary position to the maintenance of the group's integrity, as in the case of an incompetent employee who will not be discharged or a surplus of laborers who will not be laid off.[16]

The central issue in Japanese industrial organization, then, is implicitly taken as commitment to the firm, rather than as individual efficiency.

For people to collaborate in economic institutions, they must have a stable basis of relationship, and it takes a society with rather highly developed political and legal institutions for this sort of trust to develop between persons who have

[16]James C. Abegglen, "The Relationship between Economic and Social Programming in Latin America," in *Social Aspects of Economic Development in Latin America* (UNESCO, 1963), p. 266.

no other basis of mutual confidence. The relations between kin are not always amicable, but there is at least a basis from which to proceed. So kinship still persists as an important basis of economic organization in the illegal enterprises (Mafia) of the United States, where it is necessary for a group of people to trust each other in complex and large-scale economic affairs outside the protection of the formal legal system.

> If the conduct of the enterprise depends upon the maintenance of secrecy, or upon a high degree of mutual confidence, there are few guarantees as effective as the bonds of kinship. In the few trades still held secret— bell-casting, gondola-making, certain kinds of perfumery—the family organization of production has remained almost unchanged since the Middle Ages. In many parts of the world brokerage houses and other establishments engaged in the speculative branches of commerce still tend to be family affairs, based on the necessity for internal solidarity in matters of trust.
>
> It will be noted that until quite recently these special conditions were the conditions of production everywhere. Markets were overwhelmingly local, most useful skills were carefully guarded, and there were few convenient devices for enforcing contracts between strangers.[17]

A study of African businessmen points out that kinship organization has many advantages for the functioning of businesses:

> African traditions of family obligation have often been blamed for stultifying entrepreneurship—kin plunder the business of its profits, demand jobs though they are not competent, and squander its assets. The strength of the family group to assert its collective well-being over

[17]Theodore Caplow, *The Sociology of Work* (New York: McGraw-Hill Book Co., 1954), p. 251.

the prosperity of its individual members is believed to rob personal ambition of its reward and incentive. Yet equally, if once the family can identify its welfare with the progress of a business, this sense of family duty—upheld by custom and pervading every circumstance of life—turns into a powerful support. All the diffuse and unspoken obligations which bind kinsfolk together then also bind them to the business. In small concerns and great financial dynasties alike, the incorporation of a business as the mainstay of a family's continuing prosperity gives the enterprise a strength of purpose which transcends a single generation or a single household. It draws on a deeply fostered loyalty which, even when it is grudgingly extorted, no impersonal contract of employment can match. Thus if the interests of the business and the family can be made to converge, these consolidated relationships will withstand the uncertainties of a changing environment more confidently than either apart.[18]

Yet it is hard to keep the interests of the family and of the business convergent. The interviews with African businessmen in the pages that follow the above statement are eloquent as to the problems that arise in dealing with kin in a business setting, and the struggle of the businessmen to separate the firm from the economic claims of the family. The relationship between this particular aspect of the moral order and the technical order becomes altered as each evolves.

It would appear that the advantages of the kinship base most clearly outweigh the disadvantages in the formative stages of the enterprise. A study of a group of small firms in Nigeria points out that the extended family in Nigeria had a

---

[18]Peter Marris and Anthony Somerset, *African Businessmen: A Study of Entrepreneurship and Development in Kenya* (London: Routledge & Kegan Paul, 1971), p. 132.

number of positive aspects, both in increasing the supply of entrepreneurs, and in bringing together the capital for productive endeavors. Most of the small-firm entrepreneurs had been trained in the indigenous apprentice system, and, since apprentice training was expensive, most had been supported by their kin in getting the training. In addition, the greater number had been able to get capital from other kin to start the business.

> The extended family may reduce the entrepreneur's initial outlays in other ways. Family members may provide room and board, and/or building space and tools needed for the enterprise. The family may also help the fledgling entrepreneur obtain access to supplies, merchants, creditors, market authorities, local officials and persons with economic power and influence. Usually the entrepreneur does not have a formal obligation to repay family members the money expended on his training and the establishment of his firm. The lack of formal repayments may be very advantageous to the enterprise in its early years when liquid funds may be scarce.[19]

On the other hand, it seems to be hard for a firm of this sort to expand beyond a certain point: "As the income of the entrepreneur increases, the number of dependents he is required to support also increase."[20]

At this point, then, for the firms to expand there would need to take place a transition to a more bureaucratic type of organization in which the organization and finances of the firm are separated from those of the kinship group, and this may be a transition by no means easy to bring about.

[19]E. Wayne Nafziger, "The Effect of the Nigerian Extended Family on Entrepreneurial Activity," *Economic Development and Cultural Change*, 18, no. 1, pt. 1 (October 1969): 29–30.
[20]*Ibid.*, p. 31.

Whatever the long-term effects of economic development on the family, there is every reason for the new migrants to the cities of the developing world to cling to their kin, and to maximize whatever use they may make of kinship relations as a source of security, including economic security, in a world which otherwise provides them little of that. Oscar Lewis has told us at length of the difficulties of families in the slums of Mexico and Puerto Rico. But in his investigation of people from the Mexican village of Tepoztlan, who had migrated to the slums of Mexico City, he found: "Families remain strong, in fact, there is some evidence that family cohesiveness increases in the city in the face of the difficulties of city life."[21] Comparing the households of his urban sample with those back in Tepoztlan, he found that the household composition is similar to village patterns except that more extended families live together in the city.[22]

An anthropologist who studied the adaptation of a rural people, the Toba Batak, in a city of Indonesia, found that, although the forms of kinship changed in the urban setting, kinship itself took on, in a certain sense, new importance, as a vehicle for solving certain kinds of problems generic to the city. "Social relationships among urban kinsmen are generally less personal, intimate and familial than in the village."[23] The little group of people who do live together gains in contrast to the scattering of clan members, so that "the nuclear family is more important in the city than in the village."[24]

[21]Oscar Lewis, "Urbanization Without Breakdown," in *Anthropological Essays* (New York: Random House, 1970), pp. 418–19.
[22]*Ibid.*, p. 424.
[23]Edward M. Bruner, "Medan: The Role of Kinship in an Indonesian City," in *Peasants in Cities: Readings in the Anthropology of Urbanization,* ed. William Mangin (Boston: Houghton Mifflin Co., 1970), p. 132.
[24]*Ibid.*, p. 132.

On the other hand,

> the minimal lineage, which includes some members who reside in the village and others who live in the city, continues to be a meaningful cooperative corporate group. The range of the kinship system has been extended more widely in the city to encompass a larger number of more distantly related persons.[25]

There is even in the city a sort of kinship grouping that does not exist at all in the country: a clan association that functions as a mutual-aid institution in the crises of life—a birth, a death, a marriage; some even provide scholarships and loans. The situation, in summary, is as follows:

> Indonesia is a new nation that lacks a strong central government, political stability, a rapidly developing economy, and a wide extension of welfare services. In this context, kinship groups continue to serve important functions that in the established western nations have been taken over by the State or other organizations. Further . . . Medan itself is populated by many different ethnic groups which compete with one another for economic and political power. . . . One response of the urban Batak to residence in an alien and sometimes hostile environment has been to solidify lineage and kinship ties.[26]

The Toba Batak have tended "to solidify lineage and kinship ties" as a way of creating some source of security in a new nation which "lacks a strong central government, political stability, a rapidly developing economy, and a wide extension of welfare services."[27] We may suppose that it can take Indonesia some time to develop these alternative sources

[25]*Ibid.*
[26]*Ibid.*, p. 130.
[27]*Ibid.*, p. 130.

of security, and that the same may be said of many other developing nations. In the meantime—and the meantime may last a long time for the people at the bottom of the economic system—the maintenance of kinship ties in the city is more than just a lag in modernization or a sociological curiosity; it is a social and economic resource.

Poor people helping each other via the ties of kinship is no doubt a regressive and inequitable way of handling the welfare problem. But it is a way, and poor people in cities, from urban blacks in the United States to the residents of squatter settlements in developing countries, manage to stay afloat economically partly through exchange networks that are largely those of relatives.[28]

In thinking about the ways in which traditional kinship forms are likely to be modified or transformed in an industrializing society, we should be quite clear about one point: There is no reason to imagine that traditional forms will be subjected to a single set of forces, or transformed into a single "modern" family form. The developed societies are complex; groups of people within them vary in the sort and amount of resources to which they have access; to the degree that kinship forms are responsive to the resources and constraints of a given life situation, kinship forms will vary within the society.

There are likely to be pockets within the society in which corporate family groups control important chunks of resources, whether it be the special knowledge of perfumery or bellcasting, economically viable family farms, or large family-dominated corporate empires. Here the family as a corporate entity is likely to continue very much alive and well.

[28]For a review of the literature on this point, see Lisa Peattie, "The Uses of Kinship," *Reviews in Anthropology*, 3, no. 2 (March/April 1976): 142–51.

Even where the family no longer controls as an entity important economic resources, there is more than one alternative to the traditional extended family. All over the world the industrialization process seems to be generally accompanied by a shift toward a conjugal type of family, one in which the focus is on the husband–wife tie, and the nuclear family is relatively independent of other kin.[29] But this sort of nuclear, conjugal family, the one on which Parsons puts so much emphasis, is not the only potential outcome of the industrialization process.

The tightly knit nuclear family, minimizing its connections to kin outside the little group, makes every kind of sense—as Talcott Parsons points out—for the successful management of the competitive rat race. It can move as needed to further the breadwinner's career (generating of course a few problems for the wife who might want a career of her own); the family group itself becomes the guardian and manager of the status resources, which are now a critical item in a system where the family does not manage productive capital.[30]

But not everyone in a modernizing or even a modernized society is in the competitive rat race in the same sense. There are plenty of people at the bottom who have no very real hope or expectation of a career, and who have little enough status to manage that they are more concerned with staying afloat in a choppy world. People in this situation will tend to pursue a different sort of strategy; like the Toba Batak, they will, if circumstances make it at all possible, maintain a fairly wide-reaching network of kinship ties as a source of security.

[29]Goode, *The Family,* p. 108.
[30]See William H. Whyte, *The Organization Man* (New York: Simon & Schuster, 1956).

Even within the different strata at the bottom of the system, differences in the resources to be managed will tend to create related differences in family structure. Raymond Smith's study of the black family in British Guiana describes how, among people of somewhat higher levels of status, the

> occupation of the husband–father becomes significant, and there is a quite definite tendency for his position in the household group to be established and for him to become a reference point for other members of the group. . . . In the lowest status group, the only basis for male authority in the household unit is the husband–father's contribution to the economic foundation of the group, and where there are both insecurity in jobs where males are concerned, and opportunities for women to engage in money-making activities, including farming, then there is likely to develop a situation where men's roles are structurally marginal in the complex of domestic relations."[31]

Within my little neighborhood in Venezuela, it appeared that the rather undifferentiated class of "poor people" of the times before the coming of oil money was in the process of forming not a single class of "urbanites" but at least two. There was one group of families who were relatively economically secure. They had taken advantage of the new opportunities, or had been luckier, and now had a more-or-less established place within the urban system. They had acquired skill and experience in, for example, electrical work or some similar specialty, or had acquired a little income-producing property. They now had the possibility, if they took advantage of it, of saving, and of sending their children to school so that they could take advantage of future opportunities. Or

[31]Raymond Smith, *The Negro Family in British Guiana* (London: Routledge & Kegan Paul, 1956), p. 227.

they had regular jobs in the companies that gave them access to the fringe benefits and social services—health, education, housing allowances, bonuses—which reinforced the security provided in itself by a steady income.

On the other hand, there were other families in my neighborhood who were part of what is sometimes called the "secondary labor market," people without specific skills, of shifting and undependable employment, often out of work, people without a secure resource base or other form of security.

These two classes in formation, it seemed to me, were likely to be characterized by rather different kinds of kinship relations. The stability of resources and work gave the first group the basis for stability in marriage and for the nuclear family, at the same time that it provided a motive for withdrawing a little from more extended kinship ties; these would be a source of demands for aid from less succeessful individuals, a drain of resources with little compensating mutuality.

For the second group, the situation was different. They had no resources to guard, and for them, who lacked any secure position within the "official system," the only security, albeit a minimal one, was provided by ties with friends and relatives. An aunt, a cousin, was someone you might stay with on first arrival, borrow money from, cadge a meal from, leave a child with; they might ask similar help from you. These claims of kinship were not like the tie between mother and child; that was thought of as permanent, deep, irrevocable, transcending time and distance. But other kin were more than acquaintances; the tie was vulnerable to distance, to difficulty, to personal falling out—but still, there was a claim there that was more than that for nonrelatives. They were, in a very real sense, some source of security.

The result, then, was a kind of kinship structure that was

neither the corporate extended family nor the nuclear family, relatively independent of other kin. It was a set of rather individually organized kinship networks. The result also may be described as family structure which differs by social class, and which, even if responsive in the first instance to different positions in the economic structure, might in turn contribute to further class differentiation.[32]

So far, the discussion has proceeded as if the links between the family and the technical order were generally as unintended consequences of industrialization and urbanization. They are not only unplanned by government; they are sometimes deplored by policymakers. But if now we ask what kind of policy government might adopt toward the family, we must look at the linkages in a different way. If a government should decide to carry out some sort of policy toward the family, how would it do it?

What are the ways in which government action can or does affect the structure of the family?

The fact is that government policy touches the family at many points, often without deliberate intent. In Venezuela, for example, it was clear that the development agency had much more effect on "family structure" through its programs of housing development and industrial promotion—which it did not think of as an expression of family policy—than through the programs of "family life education," which the good social workers were busily developing.

Housing policy, for example, was tending to affect the extended kinship ties previously described. Within the spontaneously developed city, there was a good deal of social mixture in almost every neighborhood because there were no

[32]See Lisa Peattie, "Family and Social Network," in *The View from the Barrio* (Ann Arbor: University of Michigan Press, 1968).

exclusive "good neighborhoods" within which professionals and well-to-do merchants might segregate themselves. Furthermore, as some people at the bottom levels did well for themselves and improved their life situations, they characteristically improved their housing right where they were. The result was a great deal of social and economic heterogeneity, contact between the economically successful and the unsuccessful.

But when the planners came on the scene, they found it complicated to plan and contract for housing except in relatively homogeneous chunks—so that is what they did. As a result, the more established and upwardly mobile families in a mixed lower- and working-class neighborhood like mine had the possibility of moving into new urbanizations housing only people like themselves—and many of them did so, breaking or weakening, in the process, their ties to their less successful kin left behind.

A classic study of this kind of phenomenon is reported in the studies by Peter Willmott and Michael Young in London, of families living in the East End slums and those who had been able to move to new housing estates at the outer rim of the city. In the East End of London, these working-class families lived in rather small, and certainly physically unpretentious apartments in a long-established neighborhood. Because the neighborhood was long-established, because these were in no sense "mobile" people, and because people got an apartment, when they needed one, through a personal network of contacts, members of the same family network tended to live close by. There was a very active interchange among members of the same family, especially the women, with the sister and their Mum continually to-and-froing and taking cups of tea together; the men were somewhat at the edge of all this activity, but had their own dense interaction with other men at the local pub.[33] Now members of nuclear families from this setting were enabled, through the government housing program, to move to new housing estates in the suburbs. One might imagine that out here the same kind of life would be reestablished, but this was not so at all. The British government bureaucracy, being a modern universalist one, assigned the new housing only to certain members of a kin network, rather than helping family members to move together. The trip in to the East End from the suburbs was long and costly. The new housing was somewhat more expensive, so that even the odd sum for the man's trip to the pub was in shorter supply. The consequence was a new sort of family structure: a nuclear family, husband and wife at home or going out together, house-proud and standoffish.[34]

For these British working-class families, the economic base was solid enough for the new suburbanites to reorganize their life in a new nuclear pattern. In Lagos, a somewhat similar housing policy, applied to people without this kind of basis in the economic order, had more disastrous results. A slum-clearance policy that relocated families from the central city to new projects at the edge of the city disrupted not only their economic life—dependent as it was on access to earning opportunities in the center—but family life as well. "So far from husband and wife drawing together in a more intimate relationship they were sometimes forced to separate."[35]

In general, it seems reasonable to believe that housing

---

[33]Young and Willmott, *Family and Kinship.*

[34]Peter Willmott and Michael Young, *Family and Class in a London Suburb* (London: Routledge & Kegan Paul, 1960).

[35]Peter Marris, *Family and Social Change in an African City: A Study of Rehousing in Lagos* (London: Routledge & Kegan Paul, 1961), p. 112.

policy that makes home ownership feasible for some groups and not for others will also make for more tightly organized nuclear families in the favored groups. In the United States, for example, housing policies supporting home ownership are based on the argument that home ownership is a good thing for stable nuclear family life. We must, from this, infer that the part of the population which is too insecure economically to be eligible for home ownership has this difference added to other forces weakening the nuclear family structure at the bottom of the income scale.

Housing policy also expresses an implicit policy as to the relative weight to be placed on the public and the private sphere in life.

To take one example, a visitor to Moscow in 1964 comments on the scarcity of private apartments—with many families sharing a single apartment with another—and the way in which the lack of privacy at home contributed to a heavy use of, and interest in, the collective space of street or meeting-hall. This writer tells us:

> Transferring the center of interest of a man's life in his work to a life outside the family has basically altered his attitude towards marriage, his motive for having children, his relationship with his family. At the same time, and more important, this process occurs in reverse. Collectivity has entered family life. It has created the habit of interference with a man's privacy and subordination of his private life to the interest of the group of people with whom he lives.[36]

Lack of privacy encourages active participation in group activities, which become the primary field of activity in the

[36]Joseph Novak, *The Future is Ours Comrade* (New York: E. P. Dutton & Co., 1964), p. 32.

U.S.S.R. In the Israeli kibbutz, the regulation of the kinds of private additions to and furnishings of the private apartments are both part of the equalization of consumption and part of a continually calculated and calibrated balance of the relation between public and private life.

Another instrument for affecting the forms of the family is, of course, taxation policy. If the United States could be said to have an explicit family policy, it would be as much as anywhere expressed in its income-tax laws and in the congressional debates on these laws. The differing rates for joint returns and single persons, the deductions for dependents, the provision or failure to provide for child-care expenses as a deductible expense—all reflect conceptions of what family life should be (as, for example, what sorts of persons may be claimed as dependents), on the social desirability of children, and on the relative responsibilities of the state and of household heads for the maintenance of persons—especially, of course, children—who are not in the work force.

The begetting and rearing of children may be thought of as the action and the responsibility of parents, or it may be conceived of as the production of the future members of society, and thus as the responsibility of the whole. Indeed, it is clearly both, and from these two views flow two conflicting principles of equity in taxation and contributory social security schemes: "Individual equity ignores dependents or treats them like any other part of a man's possessions, family equity treats dependents as part-sharers in a man's income."[37] The principle of allowing deductions from taxable income for "dependents" rests on the family equity principle, the rate

[37]Margaret Wynn, *Family Policy: A Study of the Economic Costs of Rearing Children and their Social and Political Consequences* (Harmondsworth: Penguin Books, 1972), p. 197.

at which the deductions are set represents an implied sharing of responsibility between individual household heads and society as a whole.

> Countries differ widely as to how the balance of income, left after tax-free allowances, is taxed. In France, the rate of tax on this balance is much lower for the father of a family than for the childless couple or the bachelor. In the United Kingdom the balance is taxed in essentially the same way whether the income after tax is spent by the taxpayer for himself, on his wife, four children and two grandparents, or is spent by a bachelor or spinster on themselves.[38]

Similarly, the development of special schemes of social insurance and prepaid medical care for the aged implies a shifting of the responsibility for old people from their grown children to society as a whole,[39] while at the same time shifting social resources from child-rearing (and taxpaying) families to the aged.[40]

The legal system will have very important consequences for family structure, most particularly in regard to inheritance, for this will determine, in large part, the possibility for family groups to aggregate and control sets of economic resources through time, and, with this, to exert leverage over its members.

Another kind of government intervention in the family is via the development of government school systems. The system of education is bound to affect the internal structure of the family, especially when the schools put forward ideas that conflict with those held by parents, as may very easily

[38]*Ibid.*, p. 199.
[39]Alvin Louis Schorr, *Explorations in Social Policy*, Part II: *Responsibility and Family Policy* (New York: Basic Books, 1968).
[40]Wynn, *Family Policy*, pp. 268–269.

happen in the process of modernization. How will government treat this conflict? Will it adopt a policy of separating
the children, the generation of the future, as much as possible
from the influence of the past? Will it try to tie the parents
to the school and reeducate them, as, for example, has been
attempted in Tanzania? Or will it permit groups of parents
to control what the children learn in school?

Government policy can affect whether women are or are
not in the paid labor force, and this decision will certainly
make a difference to the structure of the family. So too will
the arrangements that are made for the care of children when
women work. When Senator James Buckley, speaking against
the comprehensive child-development bill in 1971, referred
to "fear that day care centers might supplant the family"[41] he
was no doubt exaggerating matters, but he had located an
important issue in government policy toward the family.

Of all the ways in which governments can play out an
implicit policy toward the family, most basic of all are probably
those that determine the structure of economic activity—large
corporate enterprises versus small firms, family farms versus
industrialized farming, and the like. The joint management
of economic resources is one of the basic foci around which
social groups, including family groups, can cohere, and the
resources, both material and immaterial, given by the system
of occupations and employment, are resources that can be
used not only in the wider social world but also in the small
interpersonal transactions of family life. But, paradoxically,
it is precisely here that governments are least likely to have
an articulated "family policy," or, at any rate, one that treats
the family as other than a means or an obstacle. When the

[41]*Congressional Record,* September 9, 1971, p. 31226.

requirements of the family as an institution are set against the requirements of economic efficiency, one always knows which will come first.

Or almost always. For, of course, with respect to any family at any time one might raise the issue of efficiency with respect to the activities we call "housework," and it is not at all clear that here economic efficiency has first place. As Theodore Caplow has said:

> By its informality, its irrationality, and its cultural importance, the whole situation of the housewife stands in violent contrast to the rest of the occupational system. . . . The system of motivation attached to the work of the housewife bears no resemblance to any other. Considering the whole range of income and status, there is a sense in which it may be said that the remuneration of a housewife is in inverse ratio to the effort demanded of her. . . . Another anomaly in the system of remuneration is the premium attached to inefficiency . . . strictly speaking, the economic functions of the housewife are interchangeable with those of the domestic servant, and literal substitution is usually possible. To avoid this menial identification (which is insupportable under the general requirement that the class status of all members of the conjugal family be the same) it is necessary to attach great importance to the difference in emotional quality between the work of the housewife and that of the servant. This device is not entirely successful. The technologically sophisticated middle class housewife continues to be aware of the identity and to question whether household drudgery (literally servant's work) is the best occupational expression she can achieve. The contrast between the highly valued activities engaged in by her husband—manipulation of symbols and personal contacts—and her own work becomes increasingly invidious as they ascend the social scale. On the other hand, the emotional aura surrounding housework is so intensified by this manner of regarding it that any rationalization

of functions (the establishment of cooperative kitchens
in housing projects, for example) is seriously hampered.[42]

It is not at all difficult to make the case that housework
is terribly inefficient. Further, it is easy to see that one aspect
of the institution of housework and of its interaction with the
monetized labor market prevailing in the rest of the economy
is the economic exploitation of women. So, it can be argued,
as it was by one radical feminist writing in the *Monthly Review*:

> Equal access to jobs outside the home, while one of the
> preconditions for women's liberation, will not in itself
> be sufficient to give equality for women; as long as work
> in the home remains a matter of private production and
> is the responsibility of women, they will simply carry a
> double work-load. A second prerequisite for women's
> liberation . . . is the conversion of the work now done
> in the home as private production into work to be done
> in the public economy.[43]

But such a policy would have its costs, and these costs
would not only be to the men who benefit both from wives
at home and from women in the labor force whose low wages
reflect the prevalence of a "secondary worker" status for fe-
males. The cost would also be the loss of a last stronghold of
personalized, unalienated work.

A few months later, another writer in the same journal
took exception to the earlier view. Pointing out the increasing
use of activities like gardening, knitting, and cooking as plea-
surable forms of self-expression, this writer proposes a different utopia, for which current housework could be seen as
precursor:

[42]Theodore Caplow, *The Sociology of Work* (New York: McGraw-Hill Book Co.,
pp. 266–68.
[43]Margaret Benston, "The Political Economy of Women's Liberation," *Monthly
Review*, 21, no. 4 (September 1969): 21.

A future in which industrial and agricultural production
is so highly developed and automated that it requires
very few people for very few hours of the day during
very few years of their lives and in which this participation in production no longer determines the social,
cultural and personal value of the individual . . . creativity in producing things with only use-value will be
more highly esteemed than individual participation in
the production of things with exchange-value.[44]

It would certainly be unreasonable to argue that the
sphere of housework is the only possible arena for nonmo-
netized activity of economic importance; it is not the only
such arena in any society, and a society which regarded it as
important that activities be carried on for other than monetary
incentives and in other than a rational economic framework
could certainly try to develop such frameworks in other areas,
as the Cuban case shows. Nor does housework have to be
the peculiar province of women, as the housework-sharing
arrangements made by some liberated couples demonstrate.
Nevertheless, housework or family work is in fact still that
area of the economic order which by its informality, its irra-
tionality and its cultural importance stands in violent contrast
to the rest of the occupational system, and it may be that it
is for precisely that reason, among others, that the family
persists as the peculiarly valued institution which it is. The
family is the prototypical little world within which persons
clearly order their affairs along lines other than the technical.
It is the last tough stronghold of those characteristics seen in
the morally ordered "folk society." Human beings cling to
such a world, even as they rebel against its constraints and
traditional inequalities, and sacrifice its traditions for eco-

[44]L. Hornstra, "On the Nuclear Family: Pro," *Monthly Review*, 22, no. 1 (May
1970): 46–49.

nomic and technical efficiency. Thus, the Women's Movement, in its struggles over the institution of housework, is
playing out in microcosm some very basic issues of social
choice.

To look at the institution of the family in the context of
development processes and development policy is to see
clearly that it is not possible to insulate the moral order from
the technical order. The development process will make use
of existing family institutions and will reshape them. The
family, our most private of institutions, is also enormously
malleable by economic forces, and affected by public policies,
even if these do not always intend the effects they have.

Family and kinship have been seen as an obstacle to
economic efficiency, as the basis for economic institutions, as
competing with the State and the realm of community, as
picking up the pieces when the economic and social systems
fail the individual. The family has been seen as the dwindling
residue of the personalistic and traditional, and as the stronghold within which personal meaning is perpetually reborn.
It is all these things. It is a means to other ends, and it may
also be seen as representing the end to which the economic
activity is a means.

Chapter 7 / EDUCATION, LEARNING, DEVELOPMENT, AND RELATED ISSUES

Work is a part of the technical order that turns out to have its basic mainsprings in the moral order, and to have, in turn, in the manner of its organization, profound consequences for the moral order. The family is an institution of the moral order that is shaped by the technical order and that constitutes an important component of technical processes. Education, on the other hand, refers to a group of social processes and to some formal and informal institutions that are located at the junction of and overlap between technical and moral orders. Because of this, education is a sticky topic and hard to deal with in development planning.

"It has now become customary to link education and ⋏

141

economic growth by emphasizing education's role in preparing the human resources needed."[1] Yes, customary, and one might think self-evident. Yet it has not always been so.

There have been whole systems of schools that have had nothing whatever to do with what is now generally spoken of as "relevance." In fact, the prototypical preindustrial school was more characteristically that which taught religious doctrine, mainly by rote, to a small group of young villagers or tribesmen, leaving the learning of such skills as hunting, farming, the working of leather, and the making of pots to quite other means of communication.

In England, at the very beginning of that industrial revolution which has ever since been the basis of comparison for all national development processes, there was considerable hostility to education for the masses. One writer stated firmly that "nineteen in twenty of the species were designed by nature for trade and manufacture," and concluded that "to take them off to read books was to do them harm, to make them not wiser or better, but impertinent, troublesome and factious."[2]

Nor was technical training, "manpower development" in the usual modern sense, an important component of the schooling even of those who were given access to schools. Indeed, for many years the training of the British ruling elite was given over to boarding schools featuring curricula stressing the translation of Latin classics and the playing of cricket; one could not claim that the socialization process represented

[1] ILO, *Towards Full Employment: A Programme for Colombia,* prepared by an Inter-Agency Team Organized by the International Labour Office ILO (Geneva: 1970), p. 215.

[2] Quoted in Christopher Hill, *Reformation to Industrial Revolution* (Harmondsworth: Penguin Books, 1969), p. 278.

by the great public schools and the playing fields of Eton was irrelevant to some useful aptitudes acquired by graduates of the system but it would be hard to make a case for the classroom's direct role in manpower production for economic growth in the sense which has now become customary.

The change that has taken place in our perception of schooling is a dual one. In the first place, schooling has come to be seen as the basic mode of technical training. An institution that began in the context of the moral integration of society was later perceived as a critical part of the technical order. In the meantime, as the political integration of citizens into the nation-state came to occupy a central role in the agenda of governments, the school as an institution came to play also a new role in the moral order, as the producer of patriotism, the seedbed of citizenship.

In the developing nations, both kinds of function are seen with special sharpness. The drive for national political integration is intense. Literacy and the spread of a national culture are critical for such integration, and the schools become the vehicle for these processes. At the same time, in the context of manpower planning, the schools come to be seen as the means for generating the technical skills needed for economic growth. The modern school that results is a very peculiar and complicated institution.

Schools have never lost their earliest function of teaching doctrine; with the rise of nationalism, the great secular religion of our times, the little religious schools were replaced or overlaid by national school systems that had as one of their functions the building of commitment to a social system wider than the village or tribe. This aspect of school does not apply only to the pupils saluting the flag or singing the national anthem within the classroom; any study of the schools in their community setting is bound to come up against schools as centers of social symbolism,[3] and one cannot observe a group of village schoolchildren ranged in the public square on some national holiday without recognizing that the school is playing an important part in a social ceremony around the themes of nationalism and modernization.

Schools are also an important part of the system of social stratification of any society. Access to formal education has much to do with access to jobs and job security, and to the possibility of social mobility between jobs and occupations, thus affecting not only individual life chances and lifetime income streams, but the general distribution of income and status. The British "old school tie" represented not so much a certification of having acquired certain particular skills as a token of having been deemed worthy of membership in, and having been socialized into, a certain status group. In Japan, the intense preoccupation of middle-class parents with their children's school performance, from kindergarden on, reflects the functioning of a system in which corporations hire, at each status level, from the graduates of particular institutions according to their prestige, and in which a man's initial entry into the occupational system after graduation pretty much determines his future career through a system of promotion dependent more on seniority than on individual performance.[4] In this aspect of their functioning, schools may be seen as the institution that legitimizes and moralizes that part of the technical order that we call the "division of labor."

---

[3]See, e.g., John R. Seeley, R. Alexander Sim, and Elizabeth W. Loosley, *Crestwood Heights: A Study of the Culture of Suburban Life* (New York: Basic Books, 1956).

[4]For a chilling description of the functioning of this system of relations between parents and children, see Ezra F. Vogel, *Japan's New Middle Class: The Salary Man and His Family in a Tokyo Suburb* (Berkeley: University of California Press, 1971).

Schools have been a way of developing labor and social discipline for the technical order. Commentators have not been lacking to point out the relationship between the rows of desks and the prominent clock in the school classroom and the social order of the factory: the school has been a way, one eighteenth-century British writer put it, in which the child could be "habituated, not to say naturalised to Labour and Fatigue."[5] Dissident movements in societies have always seen the authority structure of the schools, or, at least, of those dominated by majority interests, as a major target.

As formal education grows in extent, the educational system becomes in itself a large and direct source of employment and thus of political pressure from its employees or would-be employees. It is not merely related to the development of industry, it is an industry. Similarly, the possibility of maintaining large numbers of young persons in school has become a critical factor in the management of the labor market and of wage rates.

With access to formal education becoming a critical factor in access to "modern-sector" jobs, families all over the developing world have come to see schooling as a critical form of investment; and the location of schools has become a central issue for any sort of settlement policy. The difficulties of (or failure to) provide first-class schools in rural areas has been one of the factors drawing families out of the rural hinterland and toward the resources of the cities.

Finally, it is true that "it has become customary to link education and economic growth by emphasizing education's role in preparing the human resources needed,"[6] and to re-

[5]Quoted in E. P. Thompson, "Time, Work-Discipline and Industrial Capitalism," *Past and Present*, 38 (December 1967): 84.
[6]ILO, *Towards Full Employment: A Program for Colombia*, p. 215.

gard formal education as the critical factor in the supply
of skills in the labor force, as well as in its capacity to learn
new skills through later training or exposure to new situations.

The notion of a school system as part of a national "investment in human capital" has been called "something of
a revolution in economic thought," allowing the economics
of education to take a steadily enlarging place in the field of
economics generally, and placing the planning of education
squarely and legitimately into development planning.[7] This
revolution in thought, if such it is, is relatively recent, a matter
of the late fifties and the sixties.

In a paper summarizing the history of the concept, Mary
Jean Bowman attributes the discovery of "human capital" to
the problems that economists encountered when they tried
to explain national differences in economic performance with
the intellectual toolkit dominated by the ideas of Keynes.

> For all the variants of Keynesianism . . . shifted the
> emphasis of a whole generation of economists from
> viewing labor as an active agent of production to viewing
> labor as a passive agent that would find employment
> only if there were a high enough rate of "investment"
> and most especially of investment in the production of
> physical producer capital. Furthermore out of Keynes'
> great but ambiguous polemic . . . came some quite re-
> markable progeny—long-term "growth" theories in which
> virtually everything was explained by the amount of
> physical capital and its rate of increase.
>
> So it was that economists set themselves up for a
> series of pragmatic-political and theoretical-econometric
> shocks. For it was obvious after World War II that phys-

[7]Mary Jean Bowman, "The Human Investment Revolution in Economic
Thought," *Sociology of Education*, 39, no. 2 (Spring 1966): 112–17.

ical capital worked its miracles only in lands where there
were many qualified men who knew how to use it (The
Marshall plan countries and Japan). And the econome-
tricians discovered that their old aggregate capital/output
ratios weren't behaving properly.[8]

Another factor may have been the trend of growth in the
developed economies themselves, particularly in the case of
the United States. It was clear, in those same years after the
war, that the growing edge of the American economy was in
the management and processing of information. Peter Drucker,
looking at the United States in the late sixties, called it a
"knowledge economy":

> The "knowledge industries" which produce and
> distribute ideas and information rather than goods and
> services, accounted in 1955 for one-quarter of the U.S.
> gross national product. This was already three times the
> proportion of the national product that the country had
> spent on the "knowledge sector" in 1900. Yet by 1965,
> ten years later, the knowledge sector was taking one-
> third of a much bigger national product. In the late
> 1970's, it will account for one-half of the total national
> product. Every other dollar earned and spent in the
> American economy will be earned by producing ideas
> and information.
>
> From an economy of goods, which America was as
> recently as World War II, we have changed into a knowl-
> edge economy. What matters is that knowledge has be-
> come the central "factor of production" in an advanced,
> developed economy.[9]

Thus, a number of lines of thought seemed in the postwar
years to converge on the importance of education for the

[8]*Ibid.*, p. 117.
[9]Peter F. Drucker, *The Age of Discontinuity: Guidelines to Our Changing Society*
(New York: Harper & Row, 1968), pp. 263–64.

technical needs of economic development. There was, first, an intuitive sense that modernization meant not only mills, machinery, and roads but also skills and aptitudes to manage and develop this capital equipment, and that these skills and aptitudes required in turn a modern system of education. Second, comparisons between countries showed that the nations with high per capita production were also those with high proportions of their population enrolled in schools. Third, comparisons between firms seemed to show that those with high rates of profitability were also those that employed a high proportion of skilled and educated manpower. Fourth, economists discovered the "residual"—that is, the proportion of growth in productivity that could not be attributed simply to an increase in the inputs of labor and capital. Calculating inputs of labor and capital and comparing these with economic outputs, economists have found as much as 80 to 90 percent of increase in total output as due to the residual—presumably, the argument runs, an increase in the otherwise unmeasured skills of the labor force. The notion of the residual at once caught on among economists as a way of measuring, even if only indirectly, that part of the development process otherwise left to intuitive notions of skill and modernity. Finally, it was clear that workers with more education were receiving higher wages and salaries, and, if wages reflect the marginal productivity of labor it must then follow that schooling raises productivity at something like the same rate.

On reflection, it turns out that every one of these arguments for schooling in economic development is full of holes.[10]

[10]For critical review of the arguments, see William G. Bowen, "Assessing the Economic Contribution of Education: An Appraisal of Alternative Approaches," in *Economic Aspects of Higher Education*, ed. Seymour Harris (Paris: Organization for Economic Cooperation and Development, 1964), pp. 177–200.

The "modernity" argument is easy to debunk; the fact that developed countries have schools does not make schools the secret of their success, any more than the fact that their cities have discotheques makes discotheques the key to development. The intercountry comparison linking school enrollment ratios with GNP, besides yielding a number of ambiguities in the middle ranges, is in essence the same argument as the above, and is subject to the same objection. The correlations are there, but what is cause and what is effect? It can easily be argued that it is the wealth created by a high GNP that makes possible consumption of education, and poverty that keeps schools few, rather than the effective causality running the other way.

Comparisons between firms in the same country have somewhat similar problems of cause and effect. Those firms employing a large proportion of highly trained people also tend to be those at the frontiers of technological change, and with a great deal of market power.

As to the residual, it is certainly an argument for the importance of factors other than those of value of physical capital and number of hours worked—but just which factors? It must include economies of scale and the capacity of the developed economies to control markets through other than purely "economic" means, and, to the degree that skill is in question here, the residual gives no clue as to which skills, and how those skills are acquired. The skills must include that "management capacity" for which successful corporations are always being praised as well as capacities more strictly technical—and how much of all this is learned on the job, or absorbed out of the general stream of culture, to which schools contribute only in part, in comparison to that acquired through informal channels?

Finally, though the ability to command higher wages is

certainly an advantage that the individual derives from formal education and though there is, no doubt, a tendency for wages to reflect the marginal productivity of labor, it would be hard to argue seriously that wages, reflecting also notions of status and the differentials due to authority, collective influence on the political process, and monopoly position (often aided by formal educational credentialing), are a satisfactory index of the advances in productivity derived from a given number of years of formal education.[11]

Ivar Berg, analyzing the personnel records of a number of American corporations as to the relationship between efficiency and reliability on the job and years of schooling, got results that were at least ambiguous, and in some respect negative. He concluded that the firm belief of personnel managers in the superiority of employees with longer schooling served chiefly to enable the personnel men to use educational credentials as a convenient screening device.[12]

Developing this line of argument, it could be claimed that the existence of wage schedules differentiated according to level of formal education says nothing at all as to the effect of schooling on productivity, but merely as to the conventionalized relative claims of more or less schooled persons on the job system and thus on the distribution of society's earnings, however derived.

So we are back to our rough judgments of effects. And those judgments still seem to tell us that skill, motivation, and innovative capacity of workers and managers must be at

[11]See Barbara Wootton, *The Social Foundations of Wage Policy: A Study of Contemporary British Wage and Salary Structure* (London: George Allen & Unwin, 1955).
[12]Ivar Berg, *Education and Jobs: The Great Training Robbery* (New York: Praeger, 1970).

least as important in economic development as the presence
of physical capital, that this importance must be growing as
economies become more technologically and organizationally
complex, and that the schools must have something important
to do with developing skills, motivation, and the capacity to
innovate.

The upshot of all this is a problem for people who want
to do rational economic planning: formal education is surely
a critical part of the technical order, and should be planned
for accordingly, but there is no way of separating its technical
contribution out and measuring it in such a way as to deal
with it independently of its wider, and necessarily judgmen-
tally evaluated, social consequences.

There is no set of computations to tell us just how much
of its development budget a country should invest in education, nor what kind of education it should invest in. The
criticism leveled against "the residual" and others of the economists' arguments will not take education out of development
planning, and education, once competing with other expenditures in a development budget, should be the subject
of cost-benefit analysis. The "florescence of a new speciality
in economics"[13] called "the economics of education" is bound
to continue. But the inadequacies of narrowly economic theory in dealing with educational phenomena means that educational planning will always have to take account quite
frankly of the subtle and multiple functions that schools serve
or could be made to serve in societies that are trying to shape
their futures, and of the complex interrelationships between
formal schools and other social institutions.

One point has certainly become quite clear: the existence

[13]Bowman, "Human Investment Revolution," p. 112.

of schools will in itself make very little difference to a society that does not provide appropriate channels in which school-learning can be put to use. An anthropological study made some thirty years ago of a small Tarascan Indian community in northern Mexico furnishes a classic case study of this point.[14]

The approximately 5,000 inhabitants of the village of Cheran lived almost exclusively from a technically primitive subsistence agriculture; two storekeepers, two schoolteachers, a federal tax collector, and the town secretary constituted the small local "elite." Yet the community could not be said to be intellectually isolated; of the twenty-eight men interviewed by the writer, twenty-five had spent some time in the United States as wage laborers. He met one man who had been graduated from a high school in California. The primitive cornstalk-reed oboe of the place could be heard playing "The Beer Barrel Polka," as well as native Indian melodies.

There was also a school, in which about a quarter of the boys were enrolled. "Those who continue throughout the available course receive four years of school education. They learn to read and write and do a little simple arithmetic. They learn very little history or geography. They learn something of natural history, such as major classifications of things in the animal, mineral, and vegetable kingdoms.

"A few ambitious families send one or more of their children to high school in Morelia or to an agricultural school. Some are sent to the boarding school at Paracho where they receive some education in a trade and in farming. A few also may go to Mexico City, and a case or two were discovered of children studying law or medicine. However, it is doubtful

[14]Ralph Beals, *Cheran: A Sierra Tarascan Village* (Washington, D. C.: Smithsonian Institution, 1946).

whether two dozen families in Cheras have sent their children on to advanced school training."[15]

The relatively low school enrollments in Cheran appeared to the reporting anthropologist to be no cause for concern; it made very little difference to the local community where his interest lay.

> With all due acknowledgement of the effort and sincerity involved in the school system, the Cheran schools do not train children in any real sense for life in Cheran. The average Cheran resident completing the school training has little advantage over his unschooled fellows in following the farming routine of the community. If he can read and write he perhaps has some less chance of being swindled in business transactions and more opportunity of rising to some municipal office . . . Insofar as the education is effective and is utilized—and this is even more markedly true of those going on for more advanced education—the effect is to move the individual out of the culture of Cheran. If he stays in Cheran, he tends to become an exploiter rather than a producer, or to occupy a position where he furnishes some liaison between the rest of the population and the non-Indian world. Or, more commonly, he moves out of the Cheran culture completely, residing in some other part of Mexico. Only to a very small extent and in a very limited number of cases does an individual become a better producer, that is, a better farmer, or practice a trade learned through schools, or become a force and example guiding the community to better housing, reformed diets, better health practices or higher standards of community organization. Formal education is still not geared to the needs and problems of Cheran life.[16]

It might seem that there was a fault here in the village

[15]*Ibid.*, p. 175.
[16]*Ibid.*

school; it was providing a curriculum irrelevant to the basic conditions of rural agricultural life. But is this the conclusion to draw? We are told that

> education for life in Cheran is completely on an informal and unconscious level. Children learn first by imitating and then by doing while assisting their parents. The social and religious structure they learn little by little through observation first of parents' and later of relatives' reactions to various individuals and situations and by listening to conversations.[17]

There is no evidence that this way of acquiring "education for life in Cheran" was in any way inadequate; the technology was simple, the social and religious structure on a scale small enough to be quite accessible to this kind of learning by observation.

How would a school improve on this way of learning in the situation *as then given*? The school, in fact, represented additional kinds of skill and information that the agricultural life of Cheran had no way of putting to use; indeed, the man who had been graduated from high school in California and become a farmer like his parents led a life much like everyone else, and was indistinguishable from other Cheran subsistence farmers. The school, in fact, constituted precisely a link between the local culture of Cheran and the "national culture" of Mexico, the existence of such a link representing for Cheran itself both costs and benefits. For the individuals who went through the course of formal schooling, the experience could not add much to their abilities in a field of endeavor for which quite adequate informal training mechanisms already existed. It could merely provide the stepping-stone for social mobility to another and more generally prestigious kind of life. And

[17]*Ibid.*

from the existence of such roles, and the people who enact them, again the ordinary farmers of the village must derive both benefits and costs.

A similar theme emerges at a higher level from the growing number of reports on expensive new programs of vocational education that turn out to be practically unused by the working economies of the nations in question.[18] The typical scenario is as follows: A nation wishes to industrialize more rapidly. Educational planners see that an industrial economy needs manpower with technical interests and technical skills, and that the schools in existence are focused around literary concerns and abilities. The obvious answer is to create new secondary-level vocational and technical schools. These are then planned and put into operation, under substantial difficulties, for they turn out to require equipment and technically skilled teachers, which are naturally in short supply, for precisely the same reason that made the schools seem desirable in the first place. Because they require specialized equipment and technically skilled teachers, these schools also turn out to be very expensive—as much as nine times the cost per pupil as an ordinary secondary general school. However, they come into existence and do not lack for enrollees; this type of education seems to be in demand, and it would appear that all will soon be well.

Some study was made of the graduates of these institutions, and two rather disquieting conclusions emerged: (1) the graduates of such technical institutions are not thought by employers to be more competent than persons who never had the technical schooling but have merely had a number

[18]See summary in Burton C. Newbury and Kenneth L. Martin, "The Educational Crisis in the Less Developed Countries," *The Journal of Developing Areas*, 6, no. 2 (January 1972): 155–63.

of years of working experience, and (2), in any case, the majority of graduates are not working in jobs that utilize the expensively provided vocational training.

In Ghana, for example, 90 percent of the graduates of vocational schools become government clerks, qualifying for such jobs on the basis of the literacy component of their craft training.[19]

Similarly, a survey of employers in Tanzania showed

> a heavy consensus that the trade school graduates
> were not a desirable source of labour supply in the various craft level occupations . . . . Almost all commented
> upon the expectations of these graduates for immediate
> or very rapid promotion to foreman and supervisory
> posts—aspirations not supported by their ability to
> perform[20]

The lesson is clear; the more critical factor in any real-life educational system is not the specific content of the school curriculum but the system of opportunities and incentives that determines not only what people learn, but what use they make of whatever they have come to learn. Formal education, schooling, is only one part, in some societies very small, in others larger, of what we call socialization—the ways in which character and skill are shaped by experience in society, and in which status is defined and rewards distributed. In turn, these processes shape the way in which a system of schooling will "take."

[19]Frederick Harbison, *A Systems Analysis Approach to Human Resources Planning. Manpower and Employment Policies for Developing Countries* (Washington, D. C.: AID, 1966), quoted in Newbury and Martin, "Educational Crisis," p. 160.

[20]Robert L. Thomas, "Problems of Manpower Development," in *Tanzania: Revolution by Education,* (ed.) Idrian N. Resnick (Arusha: Longmans of Tanzania, 1968), p. 110.

In a rapidly changing society, there are many channels of educational transformation. They are both cause and effect of economic and social change: education and socialization are aspects of the various social institutions as they impinge on both children and adults, and, through adults, on their children. Some of these channels are readily influenced by government, and others less easily, indirectly, or hardly at all. But "educational planning," broadly conceived, should try to take them all into account.

Many anthropological community studies could be looked at, from this perspective, as accounts of the variety and interrelations of educational channels in simple societies. Richard Hoggart's classic *The Uses of Literacy*[21] is an account of British working-class life in much this same perspective. Hoggart knew that the British working class was educated not only in school, but in pubs, on the shop floor, through newspapers, songs, and proverbs. It would seem useful to try this approach to the educational process in developing countries, and I myself made a preliminary attempt in this direction in an account of the development process as seen from a working-class neighborhood in Venezuela.[22]

My little neighborhood was part of a rapidly growing frontier city; although the neighborhood, like many other parts of the city, was quite unplanned, the city itself was the focus of a large effort in planned development as an industrial "growth pole" in the interior. A monograph exists on the educational planning associated with the development ef-

---

[21]Richard Hoggart, *The Uses of Literacy: Aspects of Working-Class Life, with Special Reference to Publications and Entertainment* (London: Chatto & Windus, 1957).
[22]Lisa Peattie, *The View from the Barrio* (Ann Arbor: University of Michigan, 1968).

fort,[23] but for the period I shall describe (and I might say I think in good part since) the "educational planners" had relatively little to do with most of what my neighbors were learning, and how they were learning it.

My neighborhood was a very small one—less than five hundred people—isolated from the rest of the city by both natural and artificial barriers. At first glance, one might have taken it for some rural village, with its unpaved streets, where a pig or two might be seen rooting for food, lined with tiny brightly painted houses roofed with sheet aluminum or thatch.

Yet its economy was very far from that of the Mexican Indian community of Cheran. Although some families had fruit trees in their yards, or kept chickens or pigs, these constituted a negligible contribution to a local economy which was, in fact, distinctly urban. My neighbors were as dependent as anyone in the city on what they spoke of as "the companies." The largest group of wage earners were employed in the steel mill or the two iron-mining companies; others had tiny commercial enterprises (selling cloth, running tiny groceries or a local bar), or were in a variety of jobs, ranging from school teaching and accounting to washing clothes. The unemployed (and in 1962 over one third of the men had no regular jobs) had to manage with odd jobs or help from employed relatives. The people of my neighborhood were actually living from wage labor, directly or indirectly, and in the thick of the process of transformation that had been making Venezuela ever since the oil boom from a nation predominantly rural to one predominantly urban.

[23]Noel R. McGinn and R. G. Davis, *Build a Mill, Build a City, Build a School: Industrialization, Urbanization and Education in Ciudad Guayana* (Cambridge, M.I.T. Press, 1969).

They were perfectly conscious of this fact; when conversation turned to the future, they spoke of "the future of the nation" and "the future of the worker," and many parents were full of plans for their children's future in occupations quite different from their own. The ideology of progress was pervasive.

In the ideology of progress, schools and schooling had a central place. An old-man informant and friend of mine spoke of the coming of free public education in these terms: "We used to live in the darkness; now we are coming into the light." Almost all the children in the neighborhood went to school more or less regularly, and the sight of groups of children coming and going in their school uniforms made a regular rhythm to the weekday.

There was a small primary school for the first four grades in the neighborhood, but the teacher often came late and was not well regarded by parents. Those who took their children's education really seriously tended to have them enrolled in one of the larger state or nationally run schools in the town (a sort of busing at individual initiative), or, in two cases, in tuition-charging schools run by religious groups. A much smaller proportion of young people had gone on from the primary to the secondary school. When I left, several families were planning to enroll children in the just-completed technical school. Others had longer-range educational plans; a socially-aspiring nurse, herself largely self-educated, for example, intended to send her most intelligent daughter to school in Trinidad, where she could acquire, besides secretarial skills, a good command of the English language.

There were also some special courses available: technical courses for young men, and sewing and dressmaking courses for women. But these kinds of "schooling" were treated quite differently from full-time school attendance. They were treated in a utilitarian spirit, as ways of learning various spe-

cific, useful things, and carried with them no particular aura
of culture. (As to the full-time technical school I cannot speak,
for I had no opportunity to see this in actual operation, or to
observe the way in which participation in it was handled
socially.) Certainly participation in a regular primary or secondary school, and especially the "better" schools, was not
treated in a purely utilitarian spirit. One went off to school,
formally dressed in uniform, in somewhat the way one might
think of going, properly dressed, to church. The content of
the school curriculum never seemed to be evaluated or criticized by either the pupils or their parents; it was what education was. Certainly, to an outside observer imbued with
the spirit of American "progressive education," the teaching
provided seemed remarkably verbalistic and unconnected
with any active intellectual process on the part of the pupils.
One learned arithmetic (not usually applied to realistic problems), and to read, and to write neatly (by copying and taking
dictation), and one committed to memory "materials" involving a great deal of nomenclature for plants and animals,
historical facts with no depth or context, and such items as
the number of kilometers around the borders of Venezuela.

In a class of young people about to be graduated from
primary school in this city, an "industrial growth pole" to
which the government of Venezuela was committing a very
large amount of resources, I sat in on a lecture dealing with
the getting of national wealth—economic development, in
other words. The teacher had prepared thoroughly and gave
a well-prepared talk, which pupils dutifully recorded. Not
one mention was made either of industry in general, or of
any of the economic activities of the city; they were not in the
book.

In other words, the relationship that formal schooling in
my barrio had to the "technical order" was only a small part

of its function, and was largely indirect. Schooling was seen as a ritualized initiation to modern life; if one completed it successfully, it gave a certification useful for getting better jobs. It was not, to any substantial degree, a process whereby one learned how to cope with practical problems. But this did not mean that it was a trivial enterprise.

I came to understand this when I asked the members of a young men's sports club in another neighborhood to list the books that they would like to have in a local library which I was prepared to stock for them. I was not surprised to find that, like most young people, they had a keen sense for the practical, and wanted books on auto mechanics and the like, as well as some on sex education, but I was surprised to find that most of all they wanted Venezuelan classics, including poetry. When we talked this over, I saw that, for them, the last category had another kind of relevance; it meant access to elite culture, the democratizing of an intellectual monopoly. The character of the schooling provided in my community in Venezuela was not so different from that of the Mexican village of Cheran; the interest in and uses made of it were different, because the society was a very different one.

Neither the members of the boys' club nor any neighbors in general were impractical people. "Practical" skills were acquired in other ways. Although my neighbors seemed to have a rather passive relationship to the information acquired in school, their relationship to some other information streams in their environment was not passive in the least. Many of them read the news in the newspapers, and an even higher proportion listened to the news on the radio—including, I was told, a clandestine radical station—and what they heard in this way they discussed and acted upon. The fact that they did not think of themselves as having any very potent effect on national politics did not keep them from having opinions, participating in parties on the local level, and trying—sometimes quite successfully—to manipulate the local politicians in their interest. Furthermore, they were quite sophisticated as to how to make news themselves as a way of getting political leverage; confronted with some community grievance, they could go into town to the municipal hall or seek out the correspondent of the regional newspaper or the staff of the local radio station to publicize their cause.

I learned that among those of my neighbors—admittedly a minority—who had established some appreciable level of technical skill, like the electrician across the street, only a few had benefited from formal training in the specialty; this was the first generation of beneficiaries of the oil boom, in which jobs had opened up well before the nation could get a system of technical schools into operation, and the companies had, of necessity, trained men on the job. Characteristically, a bright young man had caught the eye of some American, Italian, or Spaniard, who had sponsored and trained him. One of my neighbors said of the early days of the Iron Mines Company on which our community abutted: "It was like a school. Everyone was learning."

In the process they had learned, too, how to run a union, partly through experience—the first strike at Iron Mines was a relatively unstructured "wildcat" one—and partly through men who had already been through the unionizing process in the oil camps.

Religion was also a channel of education. Most of my neighbors were nominal Roman Catholics, but neither attendance at church rituals nor intellectual understanding of its doctrines seemed very important in their lives. For a few of my neighbors, conversion to one of the Protestant Fundamentalist sects was providing another sort of education. Protestant converts, unlike Catholics, took an active role in church services, reading, testifying, discussing the Scriptures with their fellows. Furthermore to become a Protestant was to adopt a new style of life, thought of as much more demanding of self-discipline. Protestants who took the cult seriously did not drink, smoke, or dance, and generally thought of themselves as embarked on an active program of character reformation.

Contact with other sorts of role models was in itself a channel of education. The Spaniards who had emigrated to Venezuela to seek their fortunes and were running car-repair shops were a source of technical training in auto repair for those whom they employed. The example set by Italian furniture makers, I was told, had revolutionized the process of furniture-making by Venezuelans. The American staff for the companies operated from a resource base and at a social level that made them hard to emulate directly, but their whole style of life in their company-provided houses constituted for my neighbors a kind of model of "modern living."

Just as my neighbors in Venezuela were learning a great many interesting and useful things outside school, it can be shown that in developing countries generally a great deal of learning does not demand formal schools.

So one writer on the culture of the British working class suggests, from an analysis of the literacy rates in persons committed to prison, that the great drop in illiteracy rates in England came in the thirty years *before* the Elementary Education Act of 1870, rather than the thirty years after,[24] and was thus, presumably, tied as much to general social and economic changes as it was to the availability of schools *per se*. Similarly, a study of the social context of industrialization

---

[24]Robert Roberts, *The Classic Slum: Salford Life in the First Quarter of the Century* (Harmondsworth: Penguin Books, 1971), p. 130. Implied also in review of evidence by R. M. Hartwell, *The Industrial Revolution and Economic Growth* (London: Methuen & Co., 1971), pp. 236–42.

in Mexico points out that over half the literate population of Mexico in 1940 had no primary schooling, and, noting the educational role of the union in the community studied, suggests that the entrance into industry may have some important spin-off in the spread of literacy.[25] The modern mass-conscripted army may be an educational institution of very great power; rather more selectively the penitentiary is an institution for adult education (the Chilean film *The Jackal of Nahaultero* is a study, based on a real case, of the educational role of prisons).

Some governments—the Cuban case is a particularly clear example—have tried deliberately to use a wide variety of social institutions as instruments of education. Others have concentrated on schools, supplemented to a greater or lesser extent by additional educational programs—"community development," educational television, specialized study groups or courses. But in all cases, and the Cubans are no exception, formal schooling is the center of, and often effectively monopolizes, educational planning.

One could hardly sustain the position that, in devoting nearly all resources to formal schooling, the educational planners in these developing countries are simply adopting the means most ready to hand. Schools are expensive, and to get a modern system of schools into operation is an extraordinarily complicated and difficult matter. An underdeveloped nation that tries to "catch up" through schooling finds its problems compounded by problems of setting up schools where trained teachers are in scant supply, buildings lacking, and administrative institutions not in existence. This is especially true for rural areas. The problem of teachers is in many ways the hardest of all to solve in a short time. The rote

[25]Wilbert E. Moore, *Industrialization and Labor: Social Aspects of Economic Development* (Ithaca: Cornell University Press, 1957), p. 234–36.

learning and "by the book" character of schools in many underdeveloped countries is a consequence both of an elite tradition of schooling and of the lack of teachers who can do more than follow a text.[26]

Even when the schools are once in operation, they continue to be expensive to run and a heavy drain on a limited national budget with many other claims on its resources. A UNESCO report calculated that the industrialized nations, with only one-third of the world's population and only one-fourth of its young people, were in 1968 spending more than $120 billion on education, whereas developing countries spend less than $12 billion. Both developing and industrialized nations had been increasing the proportion of their GNP spent on education, but, with the developing nations having revenues that increased more slowly than those of the industrialized countries and populations that increased more rapidly, the gap was naturally increasing.[27]

It has been argued that the development of formal schooling, and the credentialing process associated with formal schooling, may even act as a brake on development by generating political pressure for make-work, essentially unproductive jobs for the professionally educated.

> Assuming, as is plausible, that the political power of the middle-class or aspiring middle-class group is greater than that of the lower-paid workers, one might anticipate an increasing tendency for policy to focus on the creation of higher-skilled and white-collar jobs, rather than lower-skilled ones. . . . And if the promotion of white-collar

[26]See Clarence E. Beeby, *The Quality of Education in Developing Countries* (Cambridge: Harvard University Press, 1966). For a particular system criticized at length from this point of view, see Rolland G. Paulston, *Society Schools and Progress in Peru* (New York: Pergamon Press, 1971).

[27]Edgar Faure *et al.*, *Learning to Be: The World of Education Today and Tomorrow* (Paris: UNESCO, 1972), p. 50.

employment consists mainly in creating inessential jobs
(as where government bureaucracy expands to sop us
the excess supply of such persons) it seems distinctly
probable that full use will not be made of the productive
capacity of those employed in this way; hence the employment policy will result in the loss of potential
output.[28]

Another argument against formal schooling is that it is
more likely than not to institutionalize social inequality. A
universal system of education cannot, after all, serve everyone
equally. Even if all children enter first grade at the age of six,
they will not all emerge from law school or some other higher
level of certification eighteen or twenty years later. People
drop out at each level, and in all societies there is a tendency
for those who start out from socially advantaged families to
stay longer on the educational escalator. Even the socialist
countries have not been immune to the tendency of those at
the top to insure their children's future by helping them to
access to the educational system. A free or heavily subsidized
system of schooling, therefore, turns out in practice to provide
a public subsidy and a publicly subsidized set of partial job
monopolies which, even if offering a social mobility route to
some, goes disproportionately to those who start out better
off.[29] This point, made for the justly admired public university
system of California several years ago,[30] is even more true for
the underdeveloped countries, where the relative scarcity of
resources for schooling tends to make the educational pyra-
mid approach the shape of an icicle with a tiny point at the

[28]R. A. Berry, "Factor Proportions and Urban Employment in Developing
Countries," *International Labour Review*, 109, no. 3 (March 1974): 217–33.
[29]See extended discussion of credentialism in Ronald Dore, *The Diploma Disease* (Berkeley: University of California Press, 1977).
[30]W. Lee Hansen and Burton A. Weisbrod, *Benefits, Cost and Finance of Public
Higher Education* (Chicago: Markham Publishing Co.), 1969.

top, and schools, in the words of Ivan Illich, "a perfect system of regressive taxation, where the privileged graduates ride on the back of the entire paying public."[31]

Illich takes the position, for this and other reasons, that schools should be abolished, and educational resources made available in individually accessed, nonsequential "learning webs." Individuals would, according to their own particular interests and in their own appropriate time, be able to find the objects, the skill models, the congenial peers, and the "educators-at-large" through whom they could educate themselves. Entrance to jobs would have to be based on skill and aptitude criteria, determined otherwise than through educational credentials.

The UNESCO report cited does not go so far as this, but it does characterize "the enduring rule of allocating most public funds for the specific benefit of the school and university population" as "fundamentally unjust," and goes on to recommend the development of nontraditional educational patterns that would break down the barriers not only between different educational disciplines, but between formal and nonformal education and make possible learning as appropriate all through an individual's lifetime; the goal of educational planning should be "a learning society."[32]

It is a long way from the human-capital theorists, manpower planners, and technocratic educational planners to the sorts of issues raised by such critics of schooling. But schools continue to be created and perpetuated, and to be the complex sorts of institutions they are because of the way all these various issues, both "moral" and "technical," interpenetrate within them. It would be hard to reconcile the total elimi-

[31]Ivan Illich, *Deschooling Society* (Harmondsworth: Penguin Books, 1973), p. 65.
[32]Faure, *Learning to Be*, p. 44.

nation of schools with several of the basic requirements of those responsible for educational planning in most developing nations: "nation building" in the political sense, and the creation of a "modern," that is, corporately organized high-technology economy, with its hierarchical management structures and its skilled specialists. Illich, who detests the national state and its efforts at nation building, and sees modern high technology as a sure road, not only to ecological crisis but also to cumulative social injustice, finds here no difficulty. The nations that want to have it both ways are in for a continuing rub.

Tanzania, trying to develop the skilled personnel to man a modernized, socialist economy, experienced student strikes that closed its trade schools in 1959 when students insisted that the task of maintaining their tools and cleaning their machines should be done for them by laborers, and in 1966 there was a sort of crisis, closing the university, when university students demonstrated against being required to perform two years of national service. Educational planners moved to tie formal schooling to manual work in farms and workshops, and to take other measures for the social and political education of the new technical elite, but so long as "There is an income pay-off for education and it gets higher as more education is acquired," and "there is virtually no pay-off for those without education,"[33] it comes about that "the logic of the market and the rhetoric of manpower planning . . . combine into a heavy brew of nascent elitism."[34]

This was, of course, the central issue in the Chinese Cul-

---

[33]Idrian N. Resnick, "Educational Barriers to Tanzania's Development," in Resnick, *Tanzania: Revolution by Education*, p. 123.
[34]John S. Saul, "High Level Manpower for Socialism," in Resnick, *op. cit.*, p. 100.

tural Revolution. For a time, the Chinese replaced academic criteria for admissions to and performance in their universities by political and social ones. Although there has been something of a swing back, the Chinese still understand the tension between "redness" and "expertness" as one that demands continual management by the institutions of education, among which they include, of course, the organizations of work.

"Education" as the acquisition of skills and shaping of attitudes is a process that goes on through all the institutions of any given society. Schools, as one kind of such institutions, are not so much specialized for educational purposes because they have, as noted, a number of other purposes as well, such as treating the educational process in a distinctive, "official," symbolically loaded way. Societies that make a strong conceptual segregation between the role of the State and those of other, "private" institutions, can, to a degree, treat formal education in schools rather separately from the rest of society, as, for example, the institutions of work. The governments of the nations that are explicitly in the business of creating a new social order cannot easily maintain such a separation. They are impelled to recognize that schools are but one of a system of interrelating institutions for the formation of skills and of consciousness, and to confront as best they can the difficulties that this interaction represents.

But, as governments everywhere extend their range of intervention, similar issues will surface with respect to educational policy, and, if public debate is permitted, will become matters of public debate. For educational planning has the potential to bring to the surface most of the hard issues of development—the balance between tradition and change and between local and wider allegiances, the relative roles of the State and the family and local community, issues of what sorts of people should get access to power and opportunity issues of the trade-offs and linkages between the needs of the technical order for skill specialization and managerial hierarchy, and the social-political drives for commitment and equality. These, we are coming to see, are the really tough issues of development policies at the national level.

Chapter 8 / DEVELOPMENT PLANNING AND THE QUALITY OF LIFE

If we now reexamine Redfield's distinction between the "moral order" and the "technical order," we see that the distinction, in many ways useful as a position from which to understand human action, represents not so much a distinction between kinds of activities as a way of representing and understanding activities. The moral order comprises the aspect of organization that involves "implicit convictions as to what is right . . . explicit ideals, or . . . similarities of conscience." The technical order is that aspect "which results from mutual usefulness, from deliberate coercion, or from the mere utilization of the same means."[1]

[1]Robert Redfield, *The Primitive World and its Transformations* (Ithaca: Cornell University Press, 1953), pp. 20–21.

But these are aspects of activities and institutions that are one in practice. Work, as the production of goods and services, is surely part of the technical order; the Cubans have organized work in terms of moral incentives, and, in so doing, suggest for our attention the social meanings and nonmaterial incentives that structure the institution of work in capitalist societies. Educational planning, as part of manpower planning and the creation of human capital, is a part of the technical order; schools are equally important as institutions of political and cultural socialization. The family is a realm of interpersonal ties, the domain *par excellence* of the moral order; but families rest on and take their structure from ties of mutual utility, and the family is part of the institutional structuring of economic activity.

The moral order is not given by the technical order, but neither is it independent of it. The Cuban system of "moral incentives" was developed as a way of solving the technical problem of mobilizing labor in the absence of consumer goods, just as much as the Papago ideal of learning to endure thirst and cold was an adaptation to an environment of scarcity and hunger.

The technical order rests also on implicit convictions as to what is right, explicit ideals, and similarities of conscience. To substantiate this statement, one would not need to look so far as Rostow's "propensity to develop fundamental science" and "propensity to seek material advance."[2] One need merely look at the role of the national state in that part of the technical order that we call "the economy." This is nowhere more evident than in the developing countries, where the development plan draws its legitimacy from nationalism, and

[2]W. W. Rostow, *The Process of Economic Growth* (New York: W. W. Norton 1962).

the state draws its legitimacy as the instrument of nation building from its role as development planner.

Indeed, looked at in this context, the very notion of development planning may appear as one of the ways in which, in our complex societies, the moral order is, in Redfield's words, "taken in charge." In our very different context it might be seen as, in some sense, the analogue of the stories which the Papago woman's father told in the dark hut. One might speak of the collective rituals associated with the development plan. If one did so, one would be debunking only because the development plan is thought of as a rational ordering of means to ends, part of the technical order; the debunking would be of the same order as when the anthropologist finds behind the witch doctor's mumbo jumbo a bit of hard-nosed practicality. Where in another society the witch doctor might feel it necessary to embellish some practical end, like the sowing of crops or the building of a canoe, with a bit of ritual, in our kind of society we like to think of ourselves, in public life at least, as rational, practical, guided by fact. "Planning" as a way of doing things implies that we are proceeding in a rational way; it casts our collective enterprises as part of the technical order.

To legitimize development planning as part of the technical order, however, it is necessary for there to be a certain underlying consensus as to goals. The objectives must also appear factual, rational. The concept of economic development as it appeared in the 1950s provided a way of formulating the objectives of national planning in an appropriate manner. In the concept of "self-sustaining economic growth," we had produced a version of the nineteenth-century idea of "progress," freed of the problematic descriptive elements. We no longer had to wonder whether it was really desirable to evolve from community to society, from organic to mechanical solidarity, from that folk society "which exhibited culture to the highest possible degree" to civilization. Instead, we had a set of material goals, on which we felt people of any culture must agree; and the progress toward these could be objectively measured as in the comparisons of gross national product and per capita income.

The legitimizing conceptualization of economic development is in trouble.

One reason why the ideology of development has lost legitimacy is to be found in the appearance of those issues that we refer to as "the ecological problem." The ideas surrounding economic development treated nature as a realm of exploitable resources; now the combination of the energy crisis and the problems of environmental pollution have raised the uncomfortable possibility that there may be physical limits to growth, and that if we do not limit growth through deliberate policy, ecological catastrophe may limit it for us.

One characteristic of our new man-made environment is rapidly increasing human population. That human species which, at its first hunting-and-gathering beginning, numbered probably fewer than ten million individuals, took a sharp upturn in its rate of increase with a greater food supply made possible by agriculture, and has been increasing still more sharply ever since the harnessing of nonbiological energy. By 1975 there were four billion human beings. There may be eight billion by 2010.

Another characteristic is an increasing use of natural resources. It is not only that there are more people; these increasing people eat up resources at an increasing per capita rate. Indeed, this increasing rate of eating up the earth is a basic aspect of that process which we used to call "progress" and now speak of as "economic growth," which is central to the functioning of our social and economic institutions, depending as they do on the maintenance of employment through the production of goods. A people that is not involved in this process as much as others is "backward." A slackening-off of the process in an "advanced country" is a depression and a national disaster.

In 1929, the worth of the gross national product (GNP) of the United States was $103.4 billion. In 1978 it was $2,106.6 billion. Even adjusting for inflation, it had more than quadrupled. It has been calculated that since 1950 the GNP has grown as much as from the landing of the *Mayflower* to 1950. This is economic growth. It is also a process by which we turn irreplaceable raw materials into old car bodies, carbon monoxide, and the rest of the trash and pollutants. This Kenneth Boulding is trying to get us to redesignate the "gross national cost."

We are beginning to have an uneasy sensation of fouling our own nest. We note uncomfortably that mother's milk in the United States now has twice the level of DDT permitted for milk shipped in interstate commerce. Barry Commoner is predicting the total pollution of our water supply or destruction of soil fertility through our pattern of fertilizers. There are even more macabre predictions; we hear of a rise of carbon dioxide in the air, doubling the CO_2 content by the year 2000, leading to a "greenhouse effect" and the melting of the polar ice caps, with consequent flooding of much of the earth. A 1968 UNESCO conference suggested that in about twenty years the earth would commence to become uninhabitable because of air pollution.

The recent political crisis over the control of the world's petroleum supply focused uncomfortable attention on the inherent limitations of the world's fossil fuel supply, and, to a somewhat lesser extent, on the inherent inefficiencies of what we think of as technical progress.

Technical progress, in the history of the human career, can be described largely in terms of the development of systems of energy transformation, of systems for converting energy from less desired forms to more desired ones—from grass to beef, from wood to heat, from coal to electricity. All these transformations are inherently wasteful; energy is used up in making the transformations. Thus, an energy system that is "efficient" at the delivery end, like electricity, is inherently inefficient in its total functioning. Thus, it has been calculated that

> in 1970 almost 10 percent of the United States useful work was done by electricity. . . . When the flow of energy from resources to end uses is charted for 1970 it is seen that producing that much electricity accounted for 26 percent of the gross consumption of energy, because of inefficiencies in generation and transmission.[3]

A country that is a "successful" example of economic growth will, therefore, consume basic fuel sources at an accelerating rate because of an increasing population increasingly demanding in the use of energy to support an increasing level of material goods with increasingly sophisticated systems of energy transformation.

> "Power corrupts" was written of man's control over other men, but it applies also to his control of energy resources. The more power an industrial society disposes of, the more it wants. The more power we use, the more we shape our cities and mold our economic and social institutions to be dependent on the applications of power and the consumption of energy.[4]

[3]Earl Cook, "The Flow of Energy in an Industrial Society," *Scientific American*, 225, no. 3 (September 1971): 136.
[4]*Ibid.*, pp. 138–140.

We have come to understand that our "advanced" technological capacity to increase food production is heavily dependent on a fossil fuel "subsidy"—to produce the chemical fertilizers, and the insecticides that many "modern" plant varieties require, and to produce and power the tractors, water pumps, and other machines we use to grow them.[5] Thus, what looks at first glance like a breakthrough in productivity is in fact yet another way in which irreplaceable capital stock is being poured into current consumption.

Americans have begun to see themselves as passengers on a small and fragile planet, a kind of Spaceship Earth. And this little ship we inhabit and overload, we share very unequally among the passengers. Robert Heilbroner puts it very neatly:

> For it is only in our time that we are reaching the limit of earthly carrying capacity, not on a local but on a global basis. Indeed, as will soon become clear, we are well past the capacity, provided that the level of resource intake and waste output represented by the average American or European is taken as a standard to be achieved by all humanity. To put it bluntly, if we take as the price of a first-class ticket the resource requirements of those passengers who travel in the Northern Hemisphere of the Spaceship, we have now reached a point at which the steerage is condemned to live forever—or at least within the horizon of the technology presently visible—at a second-level; or a point at which a considerable change in living habits must be imposed on first-class if the ship is ever to be converted to a one-class cruise. . . .
>
> To raise the existing (not the anticipated) population of the earth to American standards would require the

[5]See Howard T. Odum, *Environment, Power and Society* (New York: Wiley, Inter-science, 1971).

annual extraction of 75 times as much iron, 100 times as
much copper, 250 times as much lead, and 250 times as
much tin as we now take from the earth.[6]

Meanwhile, discussions of the quality of life in the developed countries make it clear that there is unrest even
among the first-class passengers on Planet Earth. I would not,
myself, try to argue that development has made civilized man
more unhappy than the legendary "happy savage," and I
tend to be unsympathetic to those who make the argument.
In any case, we shall never know, for all attempts to compare
happiness across time and space founder on the evident tendency of human beings to shape their satisfactions and dis-
satisfactions to what is available to them. It is hard to make
comparisons of more or less between what are such very
different *kinds* of happiness. But it does seem clear that development does not, ipso facto, produce happiness.

One problem is pointed out by Fred Hirsch in his *Social
Limits to Growth*:[7] that the satisfaction of basic needs through
economic affluence leaves people freer than ever to scramble
for relative advantage over others, and for those "positional
goods" that can by definition be accessible only to a minority
of any given population. Individualistic striving in a continually more interdependent society is bound to lead to a high
level of frustration.

Development does not satiate material needs; indeed, the
economic systems which we call "developed" would immediately break down if it did. Nor do "development" and its
concomitant "modernization" seem to fill the needs of the

---

[6]Robert Heilbroner, "Ecological Armageddon," *The New York Review of Books,*
(April 23, 1970): 3.
[7]Fred Hirsch, *Social Limits to Growth* (Cambridge: Harvard University Press,
1976).

human soul; the United States of the 1980s proliferates cults like the later Roman Empire.[8]

One symptom of the loss of legitimacy in the concept of economic growth is the popularity of criticisms like that by Schumacher, whose *Small Is Beautiful* has sold, at the time of this writing, half a million copies. Another is the myriad attempts to develop indicators of the level of living or of the quality of life. This level of adequacy may be measured in terms of a single global index, like the Gross National Product or per capita income. Or it may be measured in terms of some more differentiated set of indicators intended to represent the state of welfare (mortality and morbidity statistics, for example) or the flow through the system of goods and services (calories per capita consumed, or percent of population receiving schooling). A focus on "ecological issues" may add in some indices of air and water purity. The general style of thought is the same in any case; societies have more or less of some universally desirable goods, are further along or further behind on the path to progress. But once qualitative comparisons are at issue, attempts to make judgments as to better or worse encounter the problem that differing designs for living produce not only different levels of satisfaction, but different kinds of satisfaction, by producing people with differing values and aspirations. The comparison of cultures is in its essence a question of comparing apples and oranges. How would we compare the quality of living represented in the Papago woman's recollections of her childhood with those that I would produce from a childhood in the academic community around the University of Chicago?

---

[8]For the place of esoteric cults in contemporary developed societies see, for example, *On the Margin of the Visible: Sociology, the Esoteric and the Occult*, ed. Edward A. Tiryakian (New York: John Wiley & Sons, 1974).

To elevate a society with respect to its capacity to make possible a rich sense of meaning involves a totally different frame of reference from that which evaluates a society in terms of its capacity to produce goods and services and to prolong human life. The two kinds of societal resources are not contradictory; material resources can support a richly developed "moral order." But when we consider the societal arrangements that make possible an increasing supply of material goods, there is a contradiction. Rapid technological change brings social change, which stresses traditional belief. Physical mobility and the organization of people over wide areas break the psychic boundaries that structured the many little local groups within which peoples like the Papago could develop their own local systems of belief. The moral order that develops under these new circumstances of human life—the world religions, the national and international political movements—provide a sense of purpose, and local moral orders—the family, the local community—do not disappear, but persist in altered form. But the world we have made for ourselves is one in which doubt and dissension are bound to be the norm.

Everything we know suggests that the tightly integrated culture, in which people learn to shape their passions and projects to the resources available, requires isolation. Even at the time of the Papago woman's reminiscence, her tribe had learned to want cloth from Mexico. They were to learn to want solid houses, piped water, schools, hospitals; this set of wants is not congruent with the desire to learn how to endure cold, danger, and scarcity. The motivations that press against technical and institutional constraints to make more resources available suggest a different structure of personality and society than the motivations that are structured, as in the Papago case, around the capacity to live within tight resource constraints.

The trouble is that our situation now requires something of both of these very incompatible frameworks. We are learning that our resources as a species are, indeed, limited; we will somehow have to learn to work within limited resources. At the same time, we cannot possibly feel that our resource limits are as sharply set as the Papago saw them to be; we know that our research-and-development capacity makes it always possible that our resource limits may be pushed outward. We may be able to use minerals now too much dispersed in the earth's crust to be economically salvageable; we may grow food in the sea; we will surely do *something* that we cannot foresee specifically now.

Furthermore, we have developed the technical capacity for an intercommunication that nearly ensures that none of us will ever be in the position to settle down into some tightly integrated, sharply stylized way of life like the Papago. Our experience with technical progress suggests an absence of set resource constraints, and our contact with others continually suggests alternative ways of handling resources.

This is the context for development planning. In this context, development planning is a part of the technical order and of the moral order. It represents an effort to solve the problems that are set in the framework of "necessity or expediency." It is also one of the ways in which, in that state of human organization which Redfield called "civilization," "the moral order is taken in charge."

If, then, we reconceive the task of development planning as that of using the human capacity for social organization and for conceptualizing and forethought to deal with the human predicament, what specifically would have to be accomplished?

Heilbroner's figures, of course, assume a static technology, and a first suggestion might well be that we need technical invention that makes more efficient use of the resources now lying fallow. This is, of course, reasonable, but it seems doubtful that we can count on this strategy to solve the problem.

To address the issue outlined by Heilbroner requires, first of all, extraordinary measures for population control, policies much more effective than what we now have on hand. If we had a declining population, we would have somewhat more leeway on the other needed changes, although we would still need some; we should at least stabilize the population. How is this to occur?

We need measures of radical redistribution. I do not believe, going back to Heilbroner's ship image, that the passengers who are now jammed into the steerage are going to remain quietly below decks while the first-class passengers continue their shuffleboard above. Yet we cannot afford, our earth cannot afford, to transport the whole population of the earth in the style to which we on the upper decks are accustomed. We must stop imagining that we can plan for the whole population of the earth to "develop" on the American model. There just are not the resources. This means that we cannot accommodate the demands of people at the bottom through growth at the margins. We will have to have redistribution, and a redistribution so radical that it is difficult to imagine how it is to take place.

Suppose we take seriously the idea, now being put forward, that we should work to develop not economic growth, but rather an economy of the steady state, defined as one "in which the total population and the total stock of physical wealth are maintained at some desired levels by a minimum rate of maintenance throughout."[9]

9Herman E. Daly (Ed.), *Toward a Steady-State Economy* (San Francisco: W. H. Freeman, 1973), p. 152.

What would such an economy look like? How would it work? One thing it is likely not to be is static, noninnovative, unchanging. Even the general impression we tend to have of primitive societies as relatively unchanging is probably much exaggerated, an artifact of the data available to and the methods pursued by anthropologists. Such societies do not usually have rich historical materials, and anthropologists became used to looking at the functioning of societies and the shaping of culture at a particular time—the "anthropological present." When they became interested in change, their thought tended to treat change as the phenomenon to be explained; it is possible to treat change as more "normal." In any case, the developed societies like our own, at least if they start from somewhere like where we are now rather than from some postatomic ground zero, have too good communications and too wide a pool of cultural elements not to change and invent.

In any case, the problem set for us by the definition of a steady state economy above does not require social or cultural stasis. It requires that the "total population and the total stock of physical wealth are maintained at some desired levels." "Physical wealth" is not the whole stock of social assets, nor the whole of social production. A steady state economy seems to suggest the elaboration of nonmaterial production (arts, drama) and services. Elaboration could flower in the areas of style, and in the exploration of inner space. The production of physical goods would be held to the minimal level necessary to make possible an explosion in the "tertiary sector," which would now wholly dominate the economy.

It suggests, I think, a different balance between time and material goods than that which now prevails in the industrialized nations. We like to think of "material progress" as marked by the development of labor-saving inventions. So it is, but in the process other things are happening to human time. Time—labor time—becomes a commodity to be saved or wasted, to be separated into work and leisure. Meanwhile, growth of productivity makes time, as the economist S. B. Lindner has pointed out,[10] continually more valuable relative to material commodities. The people who are richest in commodities may thus find themselves oddly deprived in the sphere of time.

Marshall Sahlins tells us that hunter–gatherers, needing to move about over a territory as game and wild plant foods become used up in one area, become natural ascetics as to material goods; there is a "steeply diminishing utility at the margins of portability." But they have the luxury of a great deal of free time. Time used for more intensive hunting would simply use up the game faster and make it necessary to move sooner. Time used to produce goods would make more than could be carried. The result is a life that would look to any banker like a life of leisure. "Reports on hunters and gatherers of the ethnological present—specifically on those in marginal environments—suggest a mean of three to five hours per adult worker per day in food production."[11]

We have made our choices the other way. Ivan Illich calculates that "the typical American male devotes more than 1,600 hours a year to his car"—if one adds to hours of driving, and parking, those spent earning the money to pay for it and its use. "He spends four of his sixteen waking hours on the road or gathering his resources for it. . . . The model American puts in 1,600 hours to get 7,500 miles: less than five miles per hour."[12] But he has the car. We may find ourselves, as

[10]S. B. Lindner, *The Harried Leisure Class* (New York: Columbia University Press, 1970).

[11]Marshall Sahlins, *Stone Age Economics* (Chicago: Aldine-Atherton, 1972), p. 34.

[12]Ivan Illich, *Energy and Equity* (New York: Harper & Row, 1974), pp. 18–19.

physical resources get tighter, tending to consume fewer goods and to have more leisure.

From this point of view, the living arrangements referred to as the "counterculture"—probably rather misleadingly, for they seem to represent the outer edge of a general trend in the industrialized societies—do in fact constitute a sort of experimental draft of the steady state economy. They suggest what such an economy might look like: a huge elaboration of the arts of life, appreciative of rather than dominating nature, seeking adventure in the exploration of the self and of interpersonal relations, oriented toward leisure rather than the consumption of goods. And to some extent the people of the counterculture, by working on their own time and out of their own living space, have managed to create a time which, as with the Papago, is an aspect of activity not separated clearly into "work" and "recreation."

But if the counterculture is a rough outline of the future, it is only a sketch, and pretty vague around the edges. As the parents of these new subsistence farmers in New Hampshire and leatherworkers in the city like to point out, the counterculture is using the rest of a society run on very different principles. The members of the counterculture are not at all averse to driving around in vans produced on the assembly line over roads built with heavy machinery through complex administrative and financial arrangements. Although their politics may run to gut anarchism, they see no ill in applying for food stamps, and a tendency to want to see some of the world's ills and inequalities reformed may imply a need for organization on an even larger scale. (How else are we to arrange to Save the Whales?—a conspicuous campaign among members of the counterculture as I write.)

And if some reasonably complex international machinery may have to be called into play to adjudicate the interests around whales, what of the problems surrounding the current inequalities between as well as within, nations? For us, in the industrialized United States, to read the reminiscences of the Papago woman is to call up a kind of lost Eden, joining material simplicity with a sharply marked "moral order" that contrasts, for us, with all the malaises of industrial society and its discontents. For the greater part of the world's people this account would evoke only the material constraints that they are desperately trying to escape—constraints that mean in daily life not only cold and hunger and children who die of gastroenteritis but relative powerlessness in a world in which those who have dispose over those who lack.

One life-style does not a working system make. Even if we can succeed in shifting the product mix generated by our economy to one less destructive and wasteful of our global-resource base, a number of problems yet remain. These seem to be mainly in the realm of social and political organization.

The steady state economy of the Papago was the outcome of those implicit processes of struggle and necessary adjustment that made them a people of small familial groups scattered over the desert, and of the human creativity that makes virtues out of necessity. We live in societies having—as the Papago did not—the technical capability of overrunning both nature and man, and any stability we achieve is through social policy and social management, the outcome of the struggle of competing interests and the exercise of organized power. Our economies are managed economies, our societies the object of policy. If we are able to develop an economy of the steady state, we will need more organization, not less. This means that we will have to solve the problem of how that organization will work—of the moral order that fits with our kind of complicated technical order.

One reason that the steady state economy is unlikely to

be plagued by stasis is that this is evidently no easy problem to solve. What will a Presidential speech sound like in a society like this? What will people cheer for? How will discontents and internal struggles for resources be handled? For, so far, since we moved into the modern era we have handled both the problems of inequality and the need for symbols to integrate people over a whole social field through a combination of nationalism and the several versions of the idea of material progress—for in the commitment to material progress the socialist and the capitalist nations have been in agreement. What happens if material progress as we have understood it essentially stops? Issues of the quality of life and issues of equality will then plainly appear as issues to be solved in the present, rather than being left for the march of progress and development to take care of.

Thus, the very development process that made the nation-state a political possibility is likely, as it runs against its limits, to make that form of organization very difficult to manage.

Meanwhile, we can plainly see that the same problems that make old forms of organization troublesome demand new forms of organization on a larger scale still—forms which we are only barely beginning to invent. How are we to manage the politics of what has become a global economic system? Sketch versions of organizations at the global scale exist: the United Nations, the other international agencies, confederations like that of the oil-producing states, the multinational or transnational corporations. We will have to manage many interlocking worlds, from the idea of humanity down to the units that pull together for us something like what the Latin Americans call the *patria chica*, the little homeland. Just because we need organization, political and economic, at the global scale, we may need smaller levels of meaningful organization more than ever—to articulate the interests of people with little leverage at the top; to experiment with new models and new forms of action and meaning; as a frame for life at the human scale.

The revival of the small nation is one of the phenomena of our time. A professor at the University of Cologne said recently:

> It is because we ask so much of government now. We ask it to provide not only peace and prosperity but social justice, welfare, good-quality environment, happiness. There aren't any international organs for that. They do not exist. So we turn back to the only effective governments we have, national government.[13]

For many, even the nation is far too big. There is a very lively interest in the local community.

Each of these levels of organization sets problems not only of structure but of belief—the belief that infuses action with meaning, and with legitimacy. The fact that the problems to be solved are practical problems does not mean that solving them is simply a technical matter.

On the contrary, from the cargo cults of Melanesia—when whole villages threw their goods into the sea, to await the arrival of magic ships bringing all the material goods of the industrial world—to the Ras Tafarians of Jamaica, despairing of life as blacks in colonial society and looking to an earthly paradise in Ethiopia, to the managed hysteria of the Nuremberg Rallies, human beings have responded to practical stress not so much by technical action as by the production of passionate ideas.

Human beings are so constructed, it appears, as not only

---

[13]Erwin Scheech, quoted in *The New York Times* (March 23, 1975): 70.

to be able to symbolize, generalize, style, imagine, but to need to conduct their affairs in this manner. J. L. Hammond, an economic historian, reviewing the question as to whether, in the earlier stages of the British Industrial Revolution, the working class was better or worse off, finally concludes, as we might comparing the Papago woman with ourselves, that the issue is not completely referable to statistics on wages and cost of living. "On what men enjoy and what they suffer through their imagination statistics do not throw a great deal of light." Economic "progress" of the period, he says, offered to the working man neither security nor a role for self-respect and affirmation, and he sees in the working-class literature of the time "a discontent which is a revolt of the imagination." Looking at the British experience, he suggests that "To be contented a man must be able to feel that his life has another significance as belonging to the life of a world which lived before him and will survive him, belonging, that is, to the life of a world in which he is not the centre."[14]

The life of the Papago had that. The little world of the grass houses and "our relatives, all around us on the smooth flat land" had its place in the world of Coyote and Elder Brother from which visions came. Perhaps in the search for an orienting context we have permanently moved away from the supernatural world from which visions come—or perhaps not. Certainly there are other modes: especially in the realm of what we call political ideology.

We will need, as well as systems of organization, systems of belief, of attachment, of ritual that express multiple levels of working organization, and that satisfy a kind of thirst for design, which is part of the nature of the human species. The

[14]J. L. Hammond, "The Industrial Revolution and Discontent," *Economic History Review*, II, no. 2 (January 1930): 215–28.

revolt of the imagination is not an isolated event but a continually recurring human process.

The several parts of the human agenda are thus closely interconnected. The problem of species survival, and of a stable adjustment between man and nature; the problem of equality of life and the good society; and issues of meaningfulness, or the symbolic systems within which men conduct their lives; all these are tied together. To develop a stable adjustment to nature requires solving the problems of managing the economy of the steady state in its social, political, and psychological aspects. To make this work, we will have to develop appropriate systems of belief and attachment that give life meaning. We may not be able to develop that sharp savor which the Papago woman remembered when she said, "We know how to use water," but we will have to find ways, which do something for us, of what the Papago found in their search for visions and their pride in patterned endurance.

INDEX